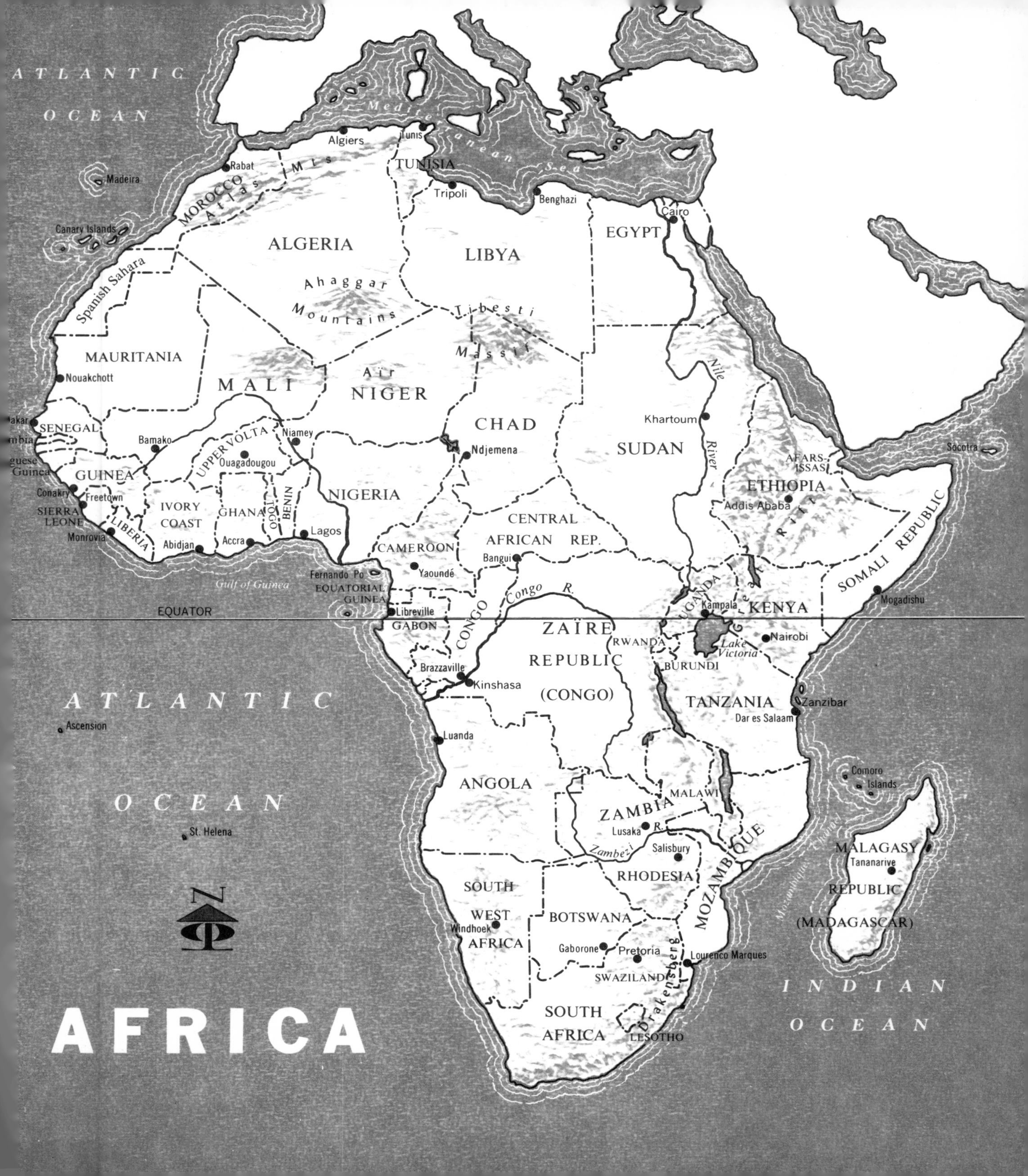
ATLANTIC OCEAN
Madeira
Canary Islands
Rabat
MOROCCO
Atlas Mts
Algiers
Tunis
TUNISIA
Tripoli
Mediterranean Sea
Benghazi
Cairo
EGYPT
ALGERIA
LIBYA
Spanish Sahara
Ahaggar Mountains
Tibesti Massif
MAURITANIA
Nouakchott
MALI
Aïr
NIGER
Red Sea
Nile River
Dakar
SENEGAL
Bamako
UPPER VOLTA
Niamey
Ouagadougou
GUINEA
Conakry
Freetown
SIERRA LEONE
Monrovia
LIBERIA
IVORY COAST
Abidjan
GHANA
Accra
TOGO
BENIN
Lagos
NIGERIA
CHAD
Ndjemena
Khartoum
SUDAN
AFARS-ISSAS
ETHIOPIA
Addis Ababa
Socotra
SOMALI REPUBLIC
Mogadishu
CENTRAL AFRICAN REP.
Bangui
CAMEROON
Yaoundé
Fernando Po
EQUATORIAL GUINEA
Gulf of Guinea
Libreville
GABON
CONGO
Congo R.
EQUATOR
UGANDA
Kampala
KENYA
Nairobi
Great Rift
Lake Victoria
ZAIRE REPUBLIC (CONGO)
RWANDA
BURUNDI
Brazzaville
Kinshasa
TANZANIA
Zanzibar
Dar es Salaam
ATLANTIC OCEAN
Ascension
Luanda
ANGOLA
Comoro Islands
MALAWI
ZAMBIA
Lusaka
Zambezi R.
Salisbury
St. Helena
MOZAMBIQUE
MALAGASY REPUBLIC (MADAGASCAR)
Tananarive
RHODESIA
SOUTH WEST AFRICA
Windhoek
BOTSWANA
Gaborone
Pretoria
Lourenco Marques
SWAZILAND
Drakensberg
INDIAN OCEAN
SOUTH AFRICA
LESOTHO
AFRICA

Enchantment of Africa

GHANA

by ALLAN CARPENTER 21,039
and JAMES HUGHES, Ph.D.

Consulting Editor
Robert Hamilton
Fellow, Department of History
Northwestern University
Evanston, Illinois

CHILDRENS PRESS, CHICAGO

THE ENCHANTMENT OF AFRICA

Available now: Botswana, Burundi, Chad, Egypt, Gabon, Ghana, Guinea, Ivory Coast, Kenya, Lesotho, Liberia, Libya, Mali, Malagasy Republic (Madagascar), Morocco, Niger, Rhodesia, Rwanda, Senegal, Sierra Leone, Sudan, Swaziland, Tanzania, Tunisia, Uganda, Upper Volta, Zaire Republic (Congo Kinshasa), Zambia

Planned for the future: Algeria, Cameroon, Central African Republic, Congo (Brazzaville), Benin (Dahomey), Equatorial Guinea, Ethiopia, The Gambia, Malawi, Mauritania, Nigeria, Somali Republic, South Africa, Togo

ACKNOWLEDGMENTS

R. Y. Anno-Okanta, Director, Public Relations Department, Republic of Ghana, Accra; F. Hayford, Counsellor/Information, Embassy of Ghana, Washington, DC; E. C. Pancoast, Public Affairs Officers, Embassy of the U.S.A., Accra; Joe Grossman, United States Information Service, Accra

Cover: Fishermen mend their nets, Allan Carpenter
Frontispiece: Designing kente cloth, Ghana Information Services

Project Editor: Joan Downing
Assistant Editor: Diane Salyers
Map Artist: Eugene Derdeyn

1 2 3 4 5 6 7 8 9 10 11 12 R 78 77

LIBRARY OF CONGRESS CATALOGING IN PUBLICATION DATA

Carpenter, John Allan, 1917—
Ghana
(Enchantment of Africa)

SUMMARY: An introduction to the geography, history, government, people, culture, resources, and major cities of Ghana.

1. Ghana—Juvenile literature. [1. Ghana]
I. Hughes, James Wilfred, 1934- joint author.
II. Title.
DT510.C37 966.7 76-41395
ISBN 0-516-04565-2

Contents

GHANA INFORMATION SERVICES

Kwame Nkrumah addresses the people of Ghana on the eve of independence.

A True Story to Set the Scene

AN INDEPENDENT BEGINNING

Prime Minister Kwame Nkrumah reached out to take the document being handed to him by British Colonial Governor Sir Charles Arden-Clarke. He quickly scanned the dispatch from London, looking for a line that would crown almost ten years of ceaseless effort. Finally he saw it in the fifth paragraph. As Dr. Nkrumah later recalled, his eyes filled with tears so that he could hardly make out the date: March 6, 1957. This, indeed, was the word for which Africa had been waiting so long.

"Waiting" was not a new feeling to Prime Minister Nkrumah. He had returned to his homeland, the Gold Coast, in 1947 to join in the efforts to establish an independent government for the Gold Coast colony. This territory, like many others, had been told that independence would be granted once the local people had established their own working government. For almost ten years now, many people of the Gold Coast had worked tirelessly to establish political parties, national goals, and a governmental structure suitable to the majority of the people. Kwame Nkrumah and his political party had received the popular support of the electorate and had finally requested a specific date from their British colonizer for the independence of the Gold Coast.

Despite the promises of the European powers, no African territory south of the Sahara had gained independence since the end of World War II in 1945. Many Africans from the Gold Coast believed their territory was long overdue for self-government. Prime Minister Nkrumah and his political party wanted independence now.

They hoped, too, that their independence would encourage other territories in Africa to pressure their colonial governments into granting independence.

On the morning of September 17, 1956, Prime Minister Nkrumah had just begun his busy day of appointments when his telephone rang. It was a call from Sir Charles. The governor told Dr. Nkrumah that an important dispatch had just been received from the British secretary of state's office. The colonial governor knew it contained an item of importance to Prime Minister Nkrumah, but he wanted the prime minister to read the document personally. Dr. Nkrumah checked his hectic schedule of the day, and noticed that he was completely occupied until three that afternoon. Despite his anxiety, Kwame Nkrumah continued his day's appointments until he was at liberty to leave his office to visit Sir Charles.

As Prime Minister Nkrumah entered the governor's office that afternoon in 1956, his heart was full of excitement. He was sure the message must concern a specific date for independence. Still, after working so hard and for so long for independence, Dr. Nkrumah could not rest comfortably until he saw the actual decree in writing.

Sir Charles greeted Dr. Nkrumah most cordially. When Dr. Nkrumah saw the smiling face of the governor, he knew in his heart what the document contained. All the years of struggle and hope were now to become a reality for the people of a new nation, to be called "Ghana." The governor extended his hand to Dr. Nkrumah to offer his congratulations. "This is a great day for you. It is the end of what you have struggled for."

For Kwame Nkrumah and the people of Ghana, March 6, 1957, was not to be the "end," but the beginning of their new nation.

That day would mark a new beginning for much of Africa as well.

The Face of the Land

Ghana is located in the western "bulge" of Africa on the Gulf of Guinea. Roughly rectangular in shape, the land covers approximately 445 miles from the Atlantic Ocean in the south to the country's border with Upper Volta in the north. Its east-west dimensions cover about 310 miles. Togo shares the eastern border with Ghana, while the Ivory Coast and a portion of Upper Volta form the western border. The

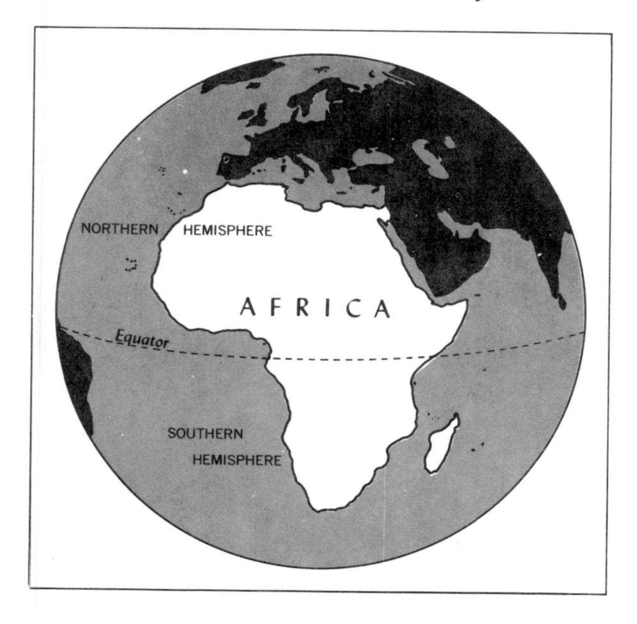

overall area of the nation is 92,100 square miles—about the size of the state of Oregon.

THE LAND

Ghana is relatively low in elevation. Along its extensive coastline on the Atlantic Ocean, the shallow waters have created a number of sandbars and beach areas. Mangrove swamps and thickets line the mouths of many rivers along the coastline. Moving into the interior, the land rises quite gradually. Slight rolling hills and valleys create a very interesting and diversified scene.

The Akwapim-Togo Range produces a striking contrast to the plains of the coastal region. These mountains, varying in height from about 1,000 feet to 2,900 feet, run in a northeasterly direction from north of Accra to the country of Togo.

In southwestern Ghana are huge, thick forest areas. Trees towering to heights of almost two hundred feet create an awesome sight. Tropical undergrowth flourishes in this moist, humid forest region.

The Kwahu Plateau is another important land feature of Ghana. Stretching about 120 miles from northwest to southeast in the central region of the nation, this plateau averages an elevation of about 1,500 feet above sea level. The Kwahu

MAP KEY

Accra, F4
Achiasi, F3
Ada, F5
Afram River, F2
Akosombo, F4
Akosombo Dam, F4
Akwapim-Togo Range, D5
Akwatia, F4
Ankobra River, F2
Axim, G2

Bamboi, D2
Bawku, A4
Berekum, E2
Bia River, F1
Bibiani, F2
Birrim River, F4
Bole, C2
Bolgatanga, B3
Bosumtwi, Lake, F3

Cape Coast, G3

Daboya, C3
Damongo, C3
Dunkwa, F3

Effiakuma, G3
Elmina, G3

Gushiago, B4

Ho, E5
Hohoe, E5

Keta, F5
Kintampo, D3
Koforidua, F4
Kpandu, E5
Kpotatufu, F5
Kujani Reserve, E4
Kulpawn River, B3
Kumasi, E3
Kwahu Plateau, E3

Lawra, B1

Mampong, E3
Mole Game Reserve, C2

Navrongo, A3
Nkawkaw, F3
Nsawam, F4
Nyakrom, F4

Obuasi, F2
Oda, F3
Ofin River, F3
Oti River, C5

Pra River, F3
Prestea, G2

Salaga, D4
Sekondi, G3
Sunyani, E2
Swedru, G4

Takoradi, G3
Tamale, C4
Tano River, F2
Tarkwa, G2
Techiman, D3
Tema, F4
Teshi, F4
Tumu, A2

Volta, Lake, D4
Volta River, F5
Volta River, Black, C3
Volta River, White, B3

Wa, B2
Wenchi, D2
Wiawso, F2
Winneba, G4

Yala, B3
Yeji, D4
Yendi, C4

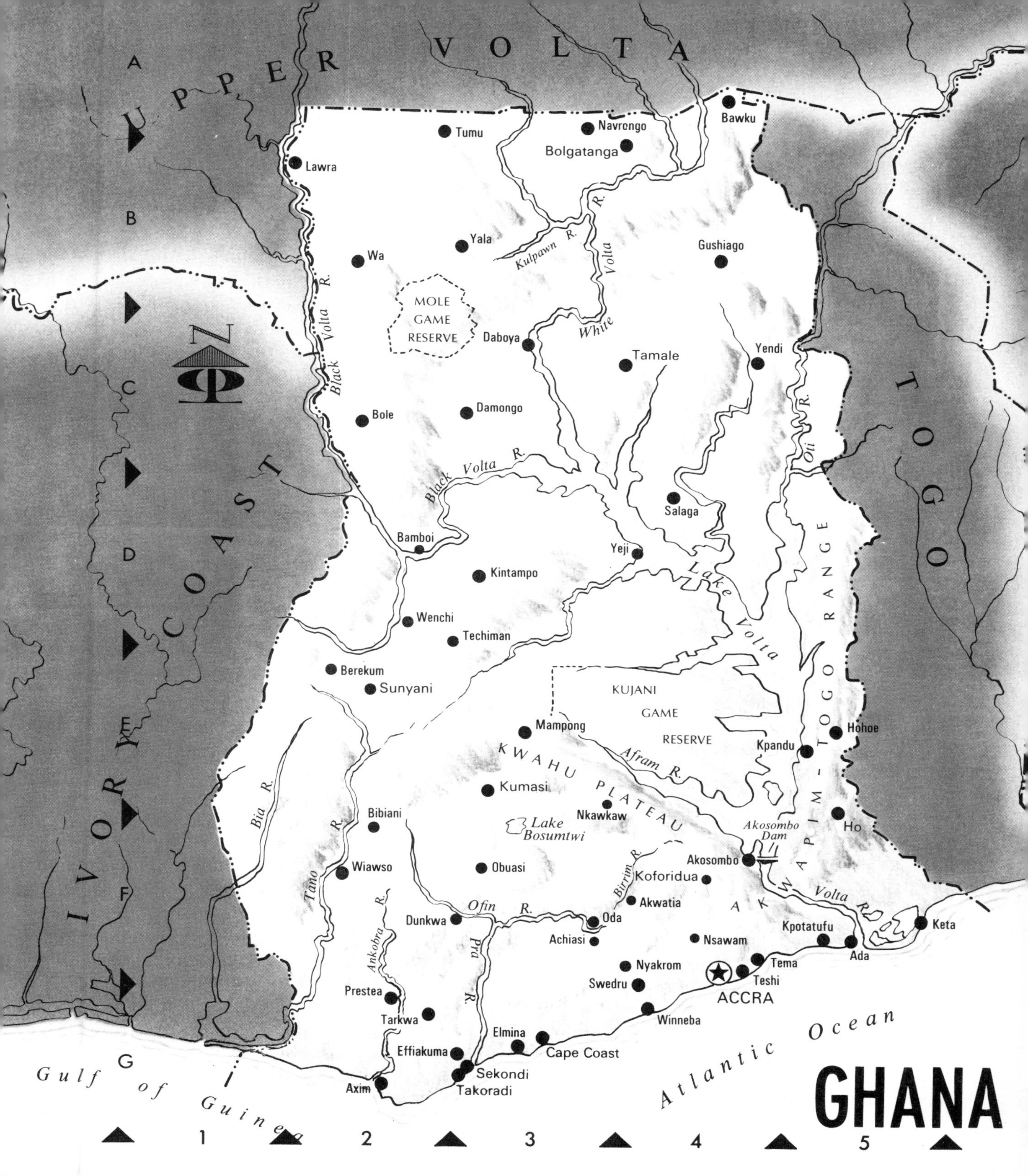
UPPER VOLTA
IVORY COAST
TOGO
GHANA
Gulf of Guinea
Atlantic Ocean
Tumu
Navrongo
Bolgatanga
Bawku
Lawra
Yala
Wa
Kulpawn R.
White Volta
Gushiago
MOLE GAME RESERVE
Daboya
Tamale
Yendi
Black Volta R.
Bole
Damongo
Oti R.
Salaga
Bamboi
Yeji
Kintampo
Lake Volta
Wenchi
Techiman
Berekum
Sunyani
KUJANI GAME RESERVE
Mampong
Hohoe
Kpandu
Afram R.
KWAHU PLATEAU
Kumasi
Nkawkaw
Bibiani
Lake Bosumtwi
Ho
Akosombo Dam
Akosombo
Bia R.
Tano R.
Wiawso
Obuasi
Birrim R.
Koforidua
Akwatia
AKWAPIM-TOGO RANGE
Volta R.
Ofin R.
Dunkwa
Oda
Achiasi
Nsawam
Kpotatufu
Keta
Ankobra R.
Pra R.
Nyakrom
Swedru
Tema
Ada
Teshi
ACCRA
Prestea
Tarkwa
Winneba
Elmina
Cape Coast
Effiakuma
Sekondi
Takoradi
Axim
A
B
C
D
E
F
G
1
2
3
4
5

Palm trees grow near the shallow waters of Ghana's Atlantic Ocean coast (right). Below: This canal irrigates farmlands on the Accra plains near Asutsuare.

THE OCEAN STEAMSHIP GROUP

UNITED NATIONS

Plateau also forms the main watershed of the country, dividing the rivers with direct Atlantic drainage from those which flow indirectly into the Atlantic via the Volta River. The plateau also forms a type of northern border for the heavily forested regions of the country. Moving northward away from this region, the land gradually becomes dry savanna.

THE WATERS

The Volta River is the most important river in Ghana. Rising in Upper Volta in the north, two principal tributaries flow southward into Ghana. The Black Volta forms part of a natural boundary between northwestern Ghana and portions of Upper Volta and Ivory Coast. The White

The Alour Hills are located near Accra, Ghana's capital city.

GHANA INFORMATION SERVICES

Volta enters Ghana in the northeast, then meanders southward until it finally joins the Black Volta to form the mighty Volta River itself.

In 1961, construction began on a dam at Akosombo, where the lengthy Volta River cut through a narrow gorge in the Akwapim-Togo Range. Although the major purpose for the dam was the production of hydroelectric power, people gave Mother Nature a bit of help in rearranging the face of Ghana's land. Water backed up from this dam has created one of the five largest man-made lakes in the world. It is called Lake Volta. The lake covers an area of about 3,500 square miles, and extends over two hundred miles upstream from the dam. This new physical feature has added much to the scenic beauty of this West African nation.

Lake Bosumtwi is another important water feature of Ghana. It is the nation's only natural lake. Located about twenty miles southeast of Kumasi, the lake has an

The Akosombo Dam on the Volta River created beautiful Lake Volta, seen here in the background.

GHANA INFORMATION SERVICES

GHANA INFORMATION SERVICES

Many small villages like this one nestle in the valleys of the Akwapim-Togo mountain range.

area of about eighteen miles and is almost 240 feet deep in parts. The land about its banks rises spectacularly from 500 to 1,400 feet. Lake Bosumtwi is an example of a "caldera" lake. It is believed that the crater in which the lake rests was formed when a volcano top either collapsed or exploded. Another theory for the creation of this deep depression is that a meteorite from space could have struck the earth here. Many tourists enjoy visiting this scenic feature.

Many other rivers add to the water network of this land. The Tano, Ankobra, Pra, and Birrim Rivers are a few of these waterways, emptying into the Gulf of Guinea.

CLIMATE AND SEASONS

The seasons in Ghana—as in most tropical countries—are divided into dry and rainy periods.

South of the Kwahu Plateau, the annual temperature averages about seventy-five to eighty-five degrees Fahrenheit. Two rainy seasons alternate with two dry seasons. Heavy rains, accompanied by winds called monsoons, come from April to July. August is dry, and lighter rains resume in September, ending in November. The months of December through March are also dry.

In the north, the temperature range is slightly greater, reaching an average high of ninety-five degrees and an average low of sixty-five degrees. The north has only one rainy season—from April to September. The rest of the year is dry. The months of November through February are especially severe in northern and eastern Ghana, for then the *harmattan* sweeps across the land. This dry Saharan wind brings red dust, which settles everywhere. The parched air sucks moisture from vegetation and the skins of animals and people. The sky becomes a red haze through which the sun shines weakly. Though the days can be excessively warm, the nights are cool.

A splendid waterfall, like this one on the Tano River near Ho, is always worthy of admiring glances.

GHANA INFORMATION SERVICES

Four Children of Ghana

TEY OF KPOTATUFU

Along the ocean in southeastern Ghana is the tiny village of Kpotatufu. Fields of grass surround the cluster of small earthen buildings that are connected by fences. In the tall grass are scattered trees and bushes. A hawk circles in the air, eyeing a small rabbit hiding beneath a bush.

In the middle of the village is the small primary school. At his desk Tey sits, restlessly looking out the window. In only a few more minutes, school will be out. Although it is only the first day of school, Tey has not been able to pay attention all day. He is thinking about his father and the other men of the village who are at the seashore, getting ready to set the large seine net that will capture many afafa (horse mackerel). Tey wishes that he, too, could be there, working with the men. Although Tey wants to be a fisherman, his father insists that he go to school.

Tey's father fishes in a boat similar to these.

MICHAEL ROBERTS

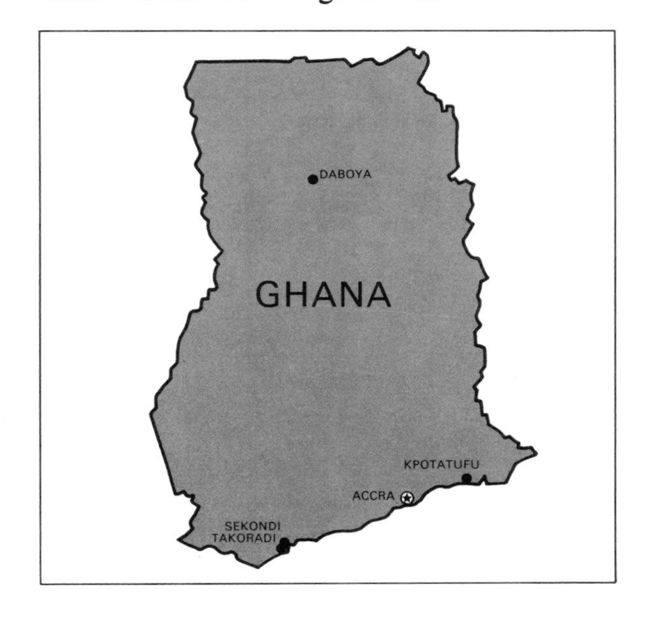

Tey thinks about last summer, when he worked by the sea with his father, except in the last weeks when it was time to harvest the shallot (green onion) crops. Then Tey and his sister helped uproot the mature shallots, pulling the green bulbs out by hand. After the plants had dried in the sun, they were tied into large bundles. Some were stored in the ceiling of the family's house, but most were sold by Tey's mother at the market in Keta, a large town to the east.

The ringing of the bell interrupts Tey from his thoughts. School is over! Tey jumps up from his desk and runs out of the building. He hardly feels the tiny drops of rain that have begun to fall.

By the time he reaches the sea, it is raining steadily. Tey sees that the men are already in their boats. From the shore, he watches them row out. When they are about half a mile out, the men throw the long, finely meshed net out of the boat in a semicircle around a school of afafa. The net is almost a mile long and sewn into a bag. A rope with lead is attached to the bottom, so the net will sink down. A long rope with corks runs through the sides of the net to keep the top afloat, so captured fish will not escape. On the ends of the net are strong ropes. The men tie these ropes to buoys out in the sea. Then the men row back to shore, pulling one end of the net with them.

By now the storm is very heavy. The wind is so strong that it is bending the trees. Waves crash onto the shore. Birds squawk excitedly and gather in groups, flying to shelter. A sandcrab races past Tey's feet, scurrying into a hole. Tey hurries under a group of trees to keep from getting soaked. He watches as the men pull the huge net behind the boat. When they reach the shore, one of the men jumps out of the canoe and ties the strong rope to a coconut tree.

Tey meets his father and together they hurry home. His mother has already prepared supper. As the family eats, Tey listens to the heavy patter of rain on the tin roof and the whistling of the wind as it passes through the trees.

When Tey awakes early the next morning, the rain has subsided. He dresses quietly and goes outside. His father is ready, too. As they walk down the muddy path, drops of rain fall from the trees. The birds chatter noisily as they hop about, looking for food.

When Tey and his father reach the sea, some men are already there. It takes nearly all the men in the village—about fifty—to pull in the huge net. And the more fish that are caught in the net, the heavier it is. Tey joins the men as they grab the rope and haul the net ashore. All the men rejoice—the net is full of fish! The village will have a feast tonight!

Top: Fishermen haul in the huge seine nets at the end of the day. Bottom: Village boys crowd around to help remove the day's afafa catch from the nets.

UNITED NATIONS

MICHAEL ROBERTS

One of Sika's favorite haunts is Takoradi's busy, bustling market.

SIKA OF TAKORADI

All the streets in the port city of Takoradi converge in the large circular marketplace—the busiest part of the city. As people crowd the walks of Takoradi, slowly heading home, a girl runs through the marketplace without stopping. Sika loves the market and usually she spends hours there. But Sika's father's ship is expected to arrive late this afternoon, and she does not want to miss it.

Sika's father is a navigator on the Black Star Line, Ghana's government-owned shipping line. His ship carries timber and other cargo to faraway ports. Usually her father's trips are to Europe, but this time the ship traveled to America—to ports on the Great Lakes. This is the longest trip her father has ever taken, and he has been gone about eight weeks. As always, Sika is anxious to hear her father's descriptions of the cities he visited. She hopes that someday she will be able to visit all the places her father has described.

As Sika reaches the dock, the sun is low in the sky. Waves are crashing on the sides of the silent ships in the harbor, and ropes squeak as the boats rock in rhythm with the water. Gulls soar through the sky with apparent ease. Black-and-white cormorants hover over the water, then dive into the waves to catch fish. Sika watches as two birds dive into the water, each coming up with one end of the same fish. She laughs as the birds fight for the fish, squawking angrily all the time. Finally one bird yanks the fish and glides away; the other bird reluctantly flies out of the water and lands on a nearby post, his eyes scanning the water for another likely catch.

Suddenly, Sika sees a ship in the distance. As the ship comes closer, Sika can make out forms on the deck. The flag of Ghana—red, yellow, and green stripes with a black star in the middle—flies high on the ship, blowing in the breeze. By now the afternoon sun is spreading its color across the blue sky. The purple waters reflect the golds and reds of the sunset.

People are beginning to arrive at the dock now, and Sika spots her mother at the other end. Sika's mother teaches at a nearby secondary school. She met Sika's father while both were attending the University of Ghana, outside the capital city of Accra. Sika hopes to be able to go there, too. But first she must go to secondary school, and to do that she must pass the secondary school exam, which she will take this year. Someday Sika would like to study medicine at the university and become a doctor, for good doctors are badly needed in the country—especially in the rural north.

The ship is close to the dock now, completely blocking the last glimpse of sun. Men throw huge ropes off the boat, and the ropes are caught by the men on the dock below. After the ropes are tied to the

A ship very much like the one Sika's father sails unloads its cargo at the Takoradi harbor.

UNITED NATIONS

UNITED NATIONS

Corn is stored in bins at this village. In the region where Mahama lives, only men are permitted to grow corn.

posts, the ladder is lowered and the men climb down, one by one. Sika spots her father and runs in that direction. She and her mother reach the ladder as Sika's father is climbing down, his duffel bag thrown over his shoulder. After hugs and hellos, the three walk down the dock, off to celebrate the homecoming.

MAHAMA OF DABOYA

Nestled in the grasslands of northern Ghana, on the bank of the White Volta River, is the little town of Daboya. It is October, and the land is wet with the rain of the past few months.

A few miles from the village, across the river, Mahama watches his cattle graze. His herd is a mixture of cattle: most are rather small, black-and-white, almost hornless cattle called West African shorthorn. There are also some larger, humped cattle called zebu. Mahama is proud of his family's many cows, for they represent status and wealth. He knows, though, that in only a month the dry season will come, parching the land. Grass will wither and the trees will lose their leaves and become stark shapes on the scorched, yellow land. Mahama is always sad during the dry season, when there is little grass for the cows to eat. Even the

GHANA INFORMATION SERVICES

Cattle are a symbol of wealth in rural West Africa. Mahama is responsible for keeping watch over his family's many cows.

White Volta shrinks to a mere stream during the dry season.

Now it is time to return home. With a stick, Mahama prods the animals on, walking behind them and watching carefully to see that they stay together. Every once in a while, Mahama must run ahead to prod a straying animal back in the right direction.

Soon dark clouds quickly cover the sky and Mahama feels the hot sun leave his body. In a matter of seconds, the rain is pouring down. As usual, the afternoon shower has come with very little warning. But though the clouds appear quickly, they disappear just as suddenly.

Mahama sees a mammy wagon on the nearby road. This brightly painted passenger truck has the name "Journey's End" painted on the rear of the vehicle. The wagon is packed with people, chickens, goats, and produce. Even from this distance, Mahama recognizes the varied sounds—laughter, crying babies, and squawking hens—as the rickety, old vehicle clatters down the road. Mahama enjoys reading the names on each mammy wagon as it passes along the roadway. One day, Mahama would like to take a trip on a mammy wagon to one of the cities in southern Ghana.

Down the road, Mahama passes the men's fields of guinea corn, millet, and groundnuts. Beyond these fields are more fields where cowpeas and bambara beans are planted. Next to the compound is the women's garden, with its rows of okra, peppers, tomatoes, and gourds.

Finally Mahama reaches the compound. A circular wall surrounds the compound, joining several round grass huts. Inside the compound are cone-shaped bins in which millet is stored. In the yard are goats, chickens, sheep, and guinea fowl, squawking and screaming. Mahama leads the cattle into the fenced yard.

Leaving the animals secure in the compound, Mahama readies himself for the evening meal. His mother has prepared a chicken-groundnut stew, which she has simmering over an open fire in the cooking area of the family compound. Her day has been an active one as well. In addition to her many preparations for the evening meal, she has also spent a good deal of time working in her garden. She smiles at Mahama, who sits upon a small stool nearby. He enjoys the spicy aroma of the stew. Soon the other members of the family will all be home together to share the meal.

AMMA OF ACCRA

Amma awoke early on the morning of August 4, 1974. In fact, she had tossed and turned all night long with excitement over the coming morning's event. This was the day when all of Ghana would adopt the new law requiring all traffic to move to the right side of the road. At 6 A.M. the new law would take effect. Amma and many others were curious and anxious to share in the morning's excitement. For a year now, Amma's father had worked with many others in Accra to help tell men, women, and children about this new law. This education program had been called "Operation Keep Right."

Amma's family has been living in the capital city of Accra for many years now. Her father originally brought the family to the city from their home village of Goaso in the Brong-Ahafo region of central Ghana. Amma remembers little of her home village, since most of her childhood memories have been associated with their family life in Accra. Since her father has been working for the government, the family will probably always stay close to the offices in Accra.

Amma has enjoyed the city life of Accra. The high-rise office complexes and shopping centers are quite an attraction for a ten-year-old. It seems as if there is always some new building being erected in

The people of Accra adjusted quickly to driving on the right side of the street.

MICHAEL ROBERTS

PRESBYTERIAN BOOK DEPOT LTD

the downtown area of the city. Often her mother takes her to visit some of the historic sites of Accra. Recently her father had taken her into the Parliament building to see the beautiful hand-carved wooden panels that decorate some of the major rooms of this important civic building. There are so many beautiful parks and buildings in and around Accra, and Amma is always eager to see new places.

Amma's brother, Ahwenee, called her that morning at 5:30 A.M. Quickly, she dressed and joined her parents and brother on the open balcony that overlooked the crowded apartment complexes on their street. It was said that at 6 A.M., all sirens, church bells, and tower chimes would ring aloud to remind everyone of the "keep right" law. In some ways Amma thought this was a humorous thing. However, her father had told Amma of the many neighboring countries that practiced "keep right" laws. It was difficult for these drivers to abide by the laws and safety practices of Ghana, and just as much a problem for Ghanaians when they drove through neighboring lands. Now all of these lands would practice the same traffic procedures.

This meant changing traffic signs from one side of the street to the other. It meant that pedestrians had to be very careful in crossing streets. Since this new law would bring traffic from a different direction, a

Cars and buses are on the "wrong" side of this Accra boulevard—but this was in the days before "Operation Keep Right" took effect.

GHANA INFORMATION SERVICES

person would be required to look to the opposite direction when crossing a street. "So many changes in one's everyday habits," said Amma's father. He was very worried for the older people who might not be able to read as well as the younger, educated citizens.

Amma's mother had hot milk-tea ready for her as she huddled close to her family all grouped together on their balcony. Suddenly the clock struck six, and the ringing began. All over the city one could hear the different bells, and car horns, and chimes, and even people with noisemakers and drums, reminding the entire population that from today on, all would "keep right."

Even bicyclists appeared confused as many of them came racing down the street and entered their first "round about." Amma was afraid someone might run into a car. One young man stopped dead in his tracks, unsure which way to go at the intersection. Even the cars pulling into service stations seemed confused as to which was the entrance, and which was the exit.

Later that day, things quieted down in the neighborhood. People did adjust quickly to the change. Amma and her girl friends walked about the neighborhood to watch the traffic at one of the major intersections. How fast things were changing, she thought. For her father, and others like him, this was just one of many changes in the new life of the people of Ghana. Who knows how many other changes Amma will face as she continues to grow up in this modern city?

Ghana Yesterday

"A NAME FROM THE PAST AS AN INSPIRATION FOR THE FUTURE"

When in late May 1956, the Gold Coast colony was readying itself for independence, the name "Ghana" was proposed for the new country.

"Ghana" had been the name of one of the first great empires of West Africa. Although the exact size of this vast empire is not precisely known, much of its territory occupied the lands of modern-day Mauritania, Mali, Senegal and Guinea.

Although this empire did not actually include the present Gold Coast, some people trace ancestral roots and traditions from parts of this territory. The new nation adopted the name of "Ghana" to express the pride of the people in this historic name as an inspiration for the future, as well as admiration for the past.

PREHISTORY

Much of the prehistory of West Africa remains a mystery. Archaeologists and geologists have only recently begun to concentrate their attentions on unravelling the riddles of early life in this part of Africa. Oral traditions, as well as some written materials of North African writers,

A nineteenth-century leader of one of Ghana's ethnic groups strikes a stiff pose for the camera.

MAC DONALD, THE GOLD COAST PAST AND PRESENT

add some additional data to life in the early years. Much more no doubt will be learned as more scholars seriously devote time to this area of African study.

Thousands of years ago, in the western section of Africa, a vast inland sea occupied part of the area today known as the Sahara Desert. Possibly as recently as 2000 B.C., natural changes began to occur which altered this once fertile region.

It is known that people used stone for tools and hunting, and early people acquired the use of fire thousands of years ago. Very early people spent much of their time hunting and gathering foodstuffs. This system of livelihood usually forced people to move about more frequently in search of their daily needs.

Later, when humans learned to grow food, rather than merely collect it, vast changes occurred in the life-styles of people. Many groups who inhabited parts of the Ghana lands in early times began to form small sedentary communities. Some no doubt raised livestock in the more suitable lands of the northern regions where grasslands were more plentiful. Even then the deadly tsetse fly was a natural limit on the degree to which livestock could successfully be tended in many parts of western and central Africa.

When iron working became more common in West Africa after 500 B.C., many changes in agricultural techniques were also possible. Iron tools and iron weapons were now more easily available to the average people, and change could occur more rapidly.

Little is known about the people who actually lived in the territory of Ghana during these very early days. Later, however, more dominant states began to develop. Outsiders began to migrate into parts of the area. They intermarried and settled within existing communities.

STRONG STATES DEVELOP

The empires of Ghana, Mali, and Songhai of central-western Africa developed, prospered, and declined while changes were occurring within the more forested regions to the south. A system of community government was evolving in the forested regions which brought people more closely together in managing their everyday problems. Agricultural developments enabled the people to produce food within dense forested regions. With the discovery of new metals, mining technology was perfected to a high degree. The commercial value of these items for trade helped unite the people of the forest lands for their own mutual benefit.

One of the early Akan states to receive attention was that of Bono. Its nearness to the gold deposits of this northwestern region made its trade highly sought after by the great empires of West Africa. It is believed that Bono began to develop about the fifteenth century, partially as a result of increased demands for gold from western and northern Africa and from Europe. Other peoples related to the Akan were also beginning to develop larger social and political units.

GHANA INFORMATION SERVICES

This carved stone head was made by people who lived in Ghana many centuries ago.

Supposedly the early Mossi people evolved a series of states in the regions now occupied by northern Ghana and southern Upper Volta. Although part of their territory was near the great Mali empire, the Mossi people are quite proud of the fact that they were never overtaken by the powerful empires north of them. They retained their independence and political stability for hundreds of years, and have remained quite faithful to their traditions.

Many other states began to evolve along the coast on the Atlantic Ocean, as well as within the interior, including the Denkyera in the southwest forest area, the Akwamu people to their southeast, and the Ga people near the site of Accra. Other branches of the Akan people, such as the Guan, Fante, and Adansi, were also emerging as united states.

GROWTH OF TRADE

By the sixteenth century, much of the land of Ghana was affected in some way by the highly developed trade routes through western Africa. Routes leading north and south connected parts of Ghana with regions of the upper Niger. Routes leading east and west provided contacts with parts of Dahomey, Togo, and Nigeria to the east, as well as to Ivory Coast and upper Guinea in the west.

The agricultural and mineral wealth were being successfully included in the trading economy of western Africa. As European explorers began to venture farther along the Gulf of Guinea, those seamen quickly established trading centers along the coast of Ghana. It was not long before this competition of coastal trade

The castle built by the Portuguese as their fort at Elmina dominates this seventeenth-century depiction of the town.

would prove troublesome to the northern trading areas which depended upon Ghana's gold and other products for part of their economy.

EUROPEAN VISITS

In the fifteenth century the Portuguese monarchs financially supported numerous voyages to the New World and Africa. Thus, between 1463 and 1481, Portuguese sailors explored most of the Guinea coast. In 1470, the Portuguese landed at a town on the Gold Coast (on the Gulf of Guinea) and obtained quantities of gold. Impressed with this wealth they named the town Da Mina (which came to be called Elmina).

In 1481, the Portuguese set forth once more for Elmina on the Gold Coast. This time they talked to the chief (probably Kwamina Ansa) of the village, requesting permission to establish a fort. Eventually their request was granted. Over the next 150 years, other settlements were established along the coast by the Portuguese.

Other Europeans competed with the Portuguese for trade along this region. Initially, the Portuguese resisted all attempts of competition by their European neighbors. However, by 1642, the Dutch had completely overtaken the Portuguese in their control of the Gold Coast. The English, as well, came to this region. So, too, did the Swedes and the Danes.

The Europeans fought over their holdings for the next two centuries: attacking each other's forts, abandoning their own, building new ones, selling or capturing or exchanging forts—all in order to monopolize trade.

During the seventeenth century the growth of plantations in America enabled another African commodity to be traded—slaves. Most slaves taken by the Dutch and the Danes came from the Gold Coast, though the heaviest slave trade was carried out farther to the west. The slave trade lasted nearly two hundred years, and at its height, possibly 10,000 people were wrenched from their homes in the hinterlands of the Gold Coast each year.

Slaves were usually supplied to the Europeans by Accra and Fante middlemen. These two groups sent agents inland to buy slaves, mostly from the Ashanti. Because Ashanti law forbade the selling of free, law-abiding citizens, most of the slaves were prisoners of war or lawbreakers. The slaves were kept in the coastal forts until boarded on ships sailing to Europe and the Americas.

Slaves are being taken to the coast and the European ships waiting there. Thousands of people were sold into slavery each year while the trade was active.

GHANA INFORMATION SERVICES

GHANA INFORMATION SERVICES

Chiefs of the great Ashanti empire sit in state while their many courtiers pay them homage.

THE ASHANTI

By the end of the seventeenth century, the Ashanti empire was beginning to emerge dramatically in the Gold Coast. Following a dispute with the Denkyera state to the south, the Ashanti gained independence from this state, and also direct access to the sea. By the mid-eighteenth century, the Ashanti empire had expanded about 150 miles from east to west and about 400 miles inland from the coast. In the process of expansion, the Ashanti formed a system of government which tried to unite all of its people. The Ashanti respected differences in customs between neighboring states, and they included these states' chiefs as part of the Assembly of the Ashanti nation.

In the history of the Ashanti empire, Osei Tutu and Okomfo Anokye were most important to the development of their strong nation. At the beginning of the eighteenth century, when the Ashanti were seeking complete independence from the Denkyera, these two men believed that the Ashanti people had to join forces to maintain a prominent position. At the time, each Ashanti group had its own chief and each chief had as his symbol of leadership a wooden stool, thought to contain the spirits of the particular group. In order to keep the various Ashanti groups united, however, Okomfo Anokye suggested that all groups be led by one major chief, who would oversee all the affairs of the Ashanti nation.

To select this Asantehene (chief of all Ashanti), the priest took three cuttings of the kuminini tree and planted one at each major Ashanti capital, Kwaman, Juaben, and Kumawu. Only the cutting planted at Kwaman lived. This was taken as a sign that Osei Tutu (the Kwaman chief) had been chosen by the gods as the head of the new nation. Kwaman then became known as Kumasi, or "under the kuminini tree."

At a great gathering in Kumasi, amid darkness and thunder, a wooden stool adorned with gold is said to have floated down from the sky onto Osei Tutu's knees. Okomfo Anokye told the chiefs that the stool contained the spirit of the Ashanti nation and that all the nation's strength and bravery depended on the safety of the stool.

This legend and Okomfo Anokye made the Ashanti conscious that they were one nation, united by a common mystical bond, symbolized by the Golden Stool. This stool still survives today, and so does the office of Asantehene.

FANTE VERSUS ASHANTI

While the Ashanti were expanding their territory and fighting their neighbors, other states were developing along the coast. During the eighteenth century, the many small Fante states joined together in an unofficial federation.

The Europeans feared a war between the Ashanti and Fante. Though the Europeans knew much about the coastal peoples, they knew practically nothing about the Ashanti. Few Europeans had ever gone inland. All they knew was that the Ashanti empire was strong and rich in gold and slaves and that the Ashanti bought guns and gunpowder.

In a dispute among chiefs, the Fante council of elders decided to shelter two Assin chiefs who opposed the Ashanti. For the first time this brought the Ashanti and Fante face to face. The balance of power on the coast depended on what would follow.

Because the Fante refused to discuss peace with the Ashanti, the Ashanti army attacked and defeated the Fante in 1807. The two Assin chiefs escaped and went to the British at Cape Coast. They convinced the British that the Ashanti were "savages." The British and Ashanti fought —for one day—until the British surrendered. The British then turned the two Assin chiefs over to the Asantehene, who responded by saying that he saw that the British were interested in trade, not in the people.

BRITISH DOMINANCE

When slavery was abolished in England in 1807, the stockholders of the British trading company (the Africa Company) faced severe losses. The merchants of the Gold Coast insisted on British military protection along the coast, while trade was maintained in mineral and agricultural products. To secure protection in the interior, it was decided that the Africa Company should seek treaties with the Ashanti nation.

In 1817 the first British mission left for the interior. The Africa Company and the Ashanti signed a treaty which stated, among other things, that no dispute remained between the Ashanti and British; that trade should be encouraged; that Ashanti traders visiting the coast would be protected; and that a British resident would be appointed to Kumasi. But the two copies of the treaty were worded differently, and each party had its own interpretation of certain words—the word "abuse," for example.

The British did not consider ridiculing someone to be an offense. But Gold Coast Africans felt differently; they were extremely sensitive to ridicule. Children were taught not to say anything that would imply ridicule or disrespect to anyone. Ridicule was then, and still is, one of the strongest sanctions in Akan law. But the British did not understand this. Thus, the treaty and its interpretations soon led to quarrels.

To clear up the confusion, a new treaty was written in 1820, but it was never ratified. Finally, the Ashanti stopped all trade with the British.

Critics in England were claiming that the Africa Company had failed in its objective—to develop a trade that would replace the slave trade. Finally, in 1821, the Africa Company was abolished, and the British government took over the handling of Gold Coast trade under Governor Charles MacCarthy. But no one told the Ashanti about the change in the system.

WAR OF 1874

In 1867, a number of critical events took place. The British and the Dutch exchanged some forts, again without consulting the local Africans. Because the local people had alliances with nearby forts, they were greatly upset by this exchange. They believed that the British and Dutch had the right to exchange forts, but not to expect the people to accept new rule against their will.

When the Asantehene, Kwaku Dua I, died in 1867, one of the first acts of his nephew and successor, Kofi Karikari, was to send forces to assist the people at Elmina. He also attacked Krepi country east of the Volta and took German missionaries as prisoners.

After taking the missionaries, the Ashanti sent three forces to the coast: one to Denkyera and Wassaw country in the west, one to the British at Cape Coast, and a third to Akim country in the east. Heavy fighting around Cape Coast resulted in a retreat by the British and their allies. However, the tide soon turned.

In January of 1874, the British, with their superior weapons, won a battle at Amoafo. Early in February, the British army reached Kumasi after heavy fighting.

GHANA INFORMATION SERVICES

In this artist's impression, British troops led by Sir Garnet Wolseley are shown entering the town of Kumasi in January 1874.

Though the city was deserted, the British troops destroyed the palace and set fire to the town as they departed.

Although the Asantehene had tried to maintain his powerful nation without succumbing to foreign powers, he soon found himself at a point of defeat. Years of battle and debate had divided his people. Some wished to separate from the overall power of the Asantehene as in older times. Confusion, disappointment, and despair reigned as these proud people were finally forced to accept the conditions of the British in February 1874. As a result, the Treaty of Fomena was signed, which greatly reduced the power of the Ashanti nation. Meanwhile, the British government decided to take more active responsibility for the Gold Coast by separating it from its charter-relationships to Sierra Leone and Lagos. Thus, the Gold Coast became a colony of England.

A PROUD NATION CONTINUES

Under Mensa Bonsu the Ashanti kingdom began to recover much of its former power. In 1883, however, he himself was deposed because of the heavy taxes he imposed. Fighting over the succession broke out and in 1887 a full-scale civil war developed. Finally, in 1888 Agyeman Prempeh became the new Asantehene.

The British in the Gold Coast had other troubles: the French were making treaties in the Ivory Coast to the west and the Germans in Togoland to the east. The British feared that the French or the Germans might increase their influence with the Ashanti.

In April 1895, William Maxwell became governor of the Gold Coast. He sent an ultimatum to the Asantehene, Agyeman Prempeh, requiring him to receive a British resident. Prempeh answered that he could not reply until he heard from his embassy in England. But the governor would not wait; he wanted to sign a treaty with the Ashanti right away.

On January 18, 1896, Governor Maxwell came to Kumasi with many troops. He told Prempeh that he would depose him unless Prempeh submitted to the queen of England and gave the governor fifty thousand ounces of gold. Slowly and silently, Prempeh slipped off his sandals (a symbolic act meaning that he was recognizing the presence of a superior), walked across the square, and embraced the feet of the governor. Prempeh said, "I now claim the protection of England." He told the governor that he was unable to pay the

Though no one was living in the town, the British burned Kumasi as they departed.

GHANA INFORMATION SERVICES

money all at once, but offered it in installments. The British then seized Prempeh, the queen mother, and many of the chiefs, taking them prisoners.

The Ashanti were amazed. Though the people protested, the troops searched the palace and royal mausoleums. When the troops found no gold, they destroyed temples and sacred trees.

YAA ASANTEWA WAR

On March 28, 1900, Governor Maxwell held a meeting of the Kumasi chiefs, saying that Prempeh would never return, that the British were now the authority in the area, and that he would call on the people to help build roads or to transport goods. The governor then demanded the Golden Stool to sit on.

This demand shocked the people. The Golden Stool was *never* sat on, under any condition. It was not a stool for the authority to sit on, as the British thought; it was a symbol of the *soul* of all the Ashanti, and the Ashanti respected it as such. The Ashanti listened to the speech in silence, then they went home to prepare for war. The people would endure British rule no longer. Three days later came the inevitable revolt, led by the queen mother of Ejisu, Yaa Asantewa.

Most of the opposition came from the Kumasi people. Governor Maxwell tried

Yaa Asantewa, shown in full battle dress, led her people in revolt against the British in March 1900.

GHANA INFORMATION SERVICES

to negotiate, but Kumasi chiefs would not accept his terms. Some Ashanti states remained neutral, while others even supported the British.

Fierce fighting continued for months. By October, however, the main Ashanti force had been broken. Small parties continued guerilla warfare, but soon they were captured. The war was over.

On January 1, 1902, Ashanti was formally annexed and placed under the authority of a chief commissioner, who was responsible to the governor. Ashanti became a British crown colony.

COLONIAL RULE

Once England gained colonial control of the Gold Coast, which included the Ashanti land, they instigated a number of developments. To improve the gold-mining activities, a railroad was constructed from Sekondi to the district of Tarkwa. As this railway line was completed to Kumasi, it reaped additional advantages for the British colonists. Not only could the colonial government insure military and political control over the interior Ashanti regions, but this railway opened up new prospects for the forest areas. Timber became a profitable export item. By 1914, the Gold Coast had become the most prosperous of all the British African colonies.

Colonial cocoa farms had an abundant supply of labor available, though minimal salaries were usually provided for the African labor. Although some medical facilities and educational institutions were begun, most of them were intended primarily for the European colonials. Some missionary groups did provide services, but for most African people of the Gold Coast, colonialism did little to advance their living standards.

INDIRECT RULE

As in other English colonies, indirect rule was encouraged within the Gold Coast. In this system, the existing local ruler was asked to carry out the laws and policy of the colonial rule. This could be done in the traditional manner, as long as the basic policy was maintained. When local rulers resisted, they could be replaced by those sympathetic with the colonial government. However, matters of national affairs were handled by the British.

TOWARD INDEPENDENCE

As British colonial rule continued, protests for an African voice in government were to be heard more and more in Ghana, as well as other regions of West Africa. In 1918, J. E. Casely Hayford, a lawyer in the Gold Coast, founded the National Congress of British West Africa to demand African participation in governmental affairs.

Another important step in the move toward independence was the launching of a popular press in the Gold Coast. Nnamdi

GHANA INFORMATION SERVICES

A meeting of the National Congress of British West Africa in London, October 1920.

Azikiwe, a Nigerian, helped launch this movement in the Gold Coast in 1935. Much work was done through this press to spread the ideas of pan-Africanism, as well as independence.

Following World War II, feeling for nationalism began to grow and spread about the continent. Many well-educated Africans were able to return to their homelands now to assist in the critical task of preparing the way for self-government. In the Gold Coast, one man to return in 1947 was Kwame Nkrumah.

KWAME NKRUMAH

Kwame Nkrumah was born in 1909 in Axim. After four years at college in Achimota, he became a teacher, then went to the United States. He graduated from Lincoln University in Pennsylvania and in 1935 entered the University of Pennsylvania. Nkrumah worked his way through college as a waiter and steward on an ocean liner, and in shipyards. After graduation, he taught for several years and then went to London, where he worked

GHANA INFORMATION SERVICES

The birthplace of Kwame Nkrumah at Axim has been specially restored.

with African students and political organizations. He developed a great interest in *pan-Africanism*—the idea of a united, independent Africa.

Secretary of the United Gold Coast Convention (UGCC) in 1947, Nkrumah broke away from the UGCC, forming his own party—the Convention People's Party (CPP). Unsatisfied with the Coussey Committee's recommendations, which proposed self-government for the Gold Coast sometime in the future, Nkrumah's platform was "self-government now."

Nkrumah wanted to bring the government to a standstill by simple noncooperation. So he called a peaceful strike and boycott in January of 1950. But during the demonstration, police fired on the people and riots broke out. Nkrumah and others were arrested and sentenced to jail for one year. The sentence, however, only heightened Nkrumah's popularity.

While Nkrumah was in prison, a new constitution that followed the Coussey Committee's recommendations was developed. A one-house legislative assembly was established, and the CPP won thirty-four of the thirty-eight assembly seats. Nkrumah was elected to the new parliament. Released from prison to take his seat, he became Leader of Government Business, then prime minister.

Nkrumah wanted all council members to be members of a political party; he wanted to exclude the local chiefs from the central government. He felt that these chiefs represented the old way—tradition, ritual, and ceremony—while the Western-educated party men represented the new, modern way.

Nkrumah obtained his long desired elective government with the constitution of 1954, which established an assembly with a speaker and 104 members. Nkrumah became prime minister (leader of the assembly). The 1954 elections gave seventy-two seats to the CPP, twelve seats to the Northern People's Party (the official opposition party), and twenty seats to independent candidates.

Africans in the north and in Ashanti felt that the CPP had become too strong. So they formed a new party, the National Liberation Movement (NLM). The NLM charged that the Nkrumah government was no longer representative of the people. Nkrumah accepted that challenge and held new elections in July of 1956. The CPP once again gained the majority of seats—72 out of 104—and Nkrumah stayed in office.

HIGH HOPES, HIGH PRICES, AND SUSPICIONS

As many people cheered the approaching days of independence, massive problems lay ahead for the government of the first new independent nation of Africa.

After World War II, prices of almost everything had risen around the world. Because the price of cocoa was high, there was much money in the Gold Coast, but there were few manufactured commodities to buy. A black market flourished, saddling Africans with very high prices for imported products.

There were problems in the cocoa industry, too. A new disease that affected cacao trees had developed. This virus disease, called "swollen shoot" and carried by the mealybug, killed the trees quickly and spread rapidly. The government demanded that farmers cut down and burn infected trees; otherwise, the cocoa industry would be destroyed. But many African farmers had never heard of tree viruses, and some did not believe that the disease could ruin the cocoa industry. They were afraid that the British just wanted to destroy the industry and steal their land.

There was little the colonial government could do to lower prices because the problem was worldwide. And the government was doing all it could to combat the swollen shoot disease. But many officials did not realize how serious the people's suspicions and problems were—because much of the government was completely out of touch with African public opinion.

The road ahead would not be easy for any government, old or new!

Ghana Today

GHANA LEADS THE WAY

The independence of Ghana was a major event in the contemporary history of black Africa. Dr. Nkrumah and his government wanted to build a model independent system that other black nationalists might wish to adopt as their territories considered the break toward independence.

It was necessary for the government of Ghana to break away from its dependency on European economic dominance, and establish its own realistic economic independence. It also needed to provide critical public services to its people. Schools were needed to help educate a citizenry that could continue to improve the standard of living in Ghana. Hospitals and social welfare agencies were needed to help care for the people who were unable to care for themselves. Highways needed to be constructed in order to bring products to and from the markets. The central railroad system needed to be extended deeper into the interior of the nation. A deep-water ocean harbor was essential to the importation and exportation of goods in Ghana. The necessity for cheaper power required the expensive construction of the Volta Dam, which was completed by 1965. Although these developments

Kwame Nkrumah smiles with former president Masemba-Débat of Congo (Brazzaville).

GHANA INFORMATION SERVICES

UNITED NATIONS

Above: Christianborg Castle, the government house, as it appeared in 1958. Opposite, top: Kwame Nkrumah (seated at left) and other government leaders officially open Ghana's parliament. Opposite, bottom: The State House in Accra was formally opened in 1957.

were ambitious, they were considered necessary by many people if Ghana was to take its place in the modern world.

Along with these moves came changes in the structure of the government. In 1960, the government adopted a republican constitution that strengthened the executive branch, establishing a president and parliament, each elected for five-year terms. At election time, each parliamentary candidate would declare which presidential candidate he would support. The president would choose cabinet ministers from parliament. Dr. Nkrumah continued to lead the government of Ghana.

PROBLEMS, POLITICAL AND ECONOMIC

While Dr. Nkrumah was on a tour abroad in September 1961, railroad, port, and bus workers went on strike. A limited state of emergency was declared. When the president returned, he appealed to workers to return to their jobs. They finally did—only after the second appeal. Dr. Nkrumah and other CPP leaders believed that the United Party had organized the strike. The UP was an opposition party composed of many regional political groups. In 1961, the Legislative Assembly

GHANA INFORMATION SERVICES

passed resolutions making Ghana a one-party state.

Political tension increased when a number of attempts were made on Nkrumah's life. An atmosphere of terror and discontent reigned in Ghana. The country had spent its reserve money in the eight years since independence; the price of food had risen and the poor were suffering; everyone was afraid of being denounced as an informer and of being sent to prison; Nkrumah's political opponents had already been exiled or imprisoned.

In February 1966, Nkrumah made a state visit to Peking, capital of the People's Republic of China, taking along sixty officials. While he was away, on February 24, a group of army officers successfully carried out a *coup d'état.* The National Liberation Council (NLC) was set up, headed by General Joseph A. Ankrah.

Dr. Kofi Abrefa Busia and other political exiles returned home. Detention camps were broken up. The NLC declared that a new constitution would be drafted and submitted to a referendum as soon as possible. Military rule lasted for three years, however; during that time the NLC attempted to stabilize the economy.

In August 1969, a new constitution was adopted, providing for a parliamentary form of government with three governmental branches. The president, elected for a four-year term, had mostly ceremonial functions and very little actual power. He was aided by the Council of State. The Cabinet had 16 members. The National Assembly, or legislative branch, was composed of 140 to 150 members; the leader of the party that won the most assembly seats became prime minister, or head of the government. The prime minister and assembly members were elected for five-year terms. The Supreme Court, or judicial branch, was headed by the chief justice, who was appointed by the president. As a result of this new constitution, Kofi A. Busia was elected prime minister of the nation. It was now his turn to try and improve the situation in Ghana.

BUSIA

Dr. Kofi Abrefa Busia, born in 1913, grew up in Wenchi. He taught at Wesley College at Kumasi and was appointed to the staff of Prince of Wales College in Achimota in 1936. Three years later, he received a degree in history at London University and won a scholarship to Oxford.

One of the first two Africans to be appointed to the Gold Coast's administrative service, Busia became assistant district commissioner in 1942. Later he returned to Oxford, where he received a Ph.D. degree. In 1949, Dr. Busia became the head of the Department of Sociology at the new University College of the Gold Coast (now the University of Ghana). Two years later, he was elected to the Gold Coast Legislative Assembly.

Although Dr. Busia was not attracted to politics, he entered the field because he

Right: Dr. Kofi Abrefa Busia, who was elected prime minister of Ghana in 1969. Below: Voters cast their ballots at the 1969 general elections.

GHANA INFORMATION SERVICES

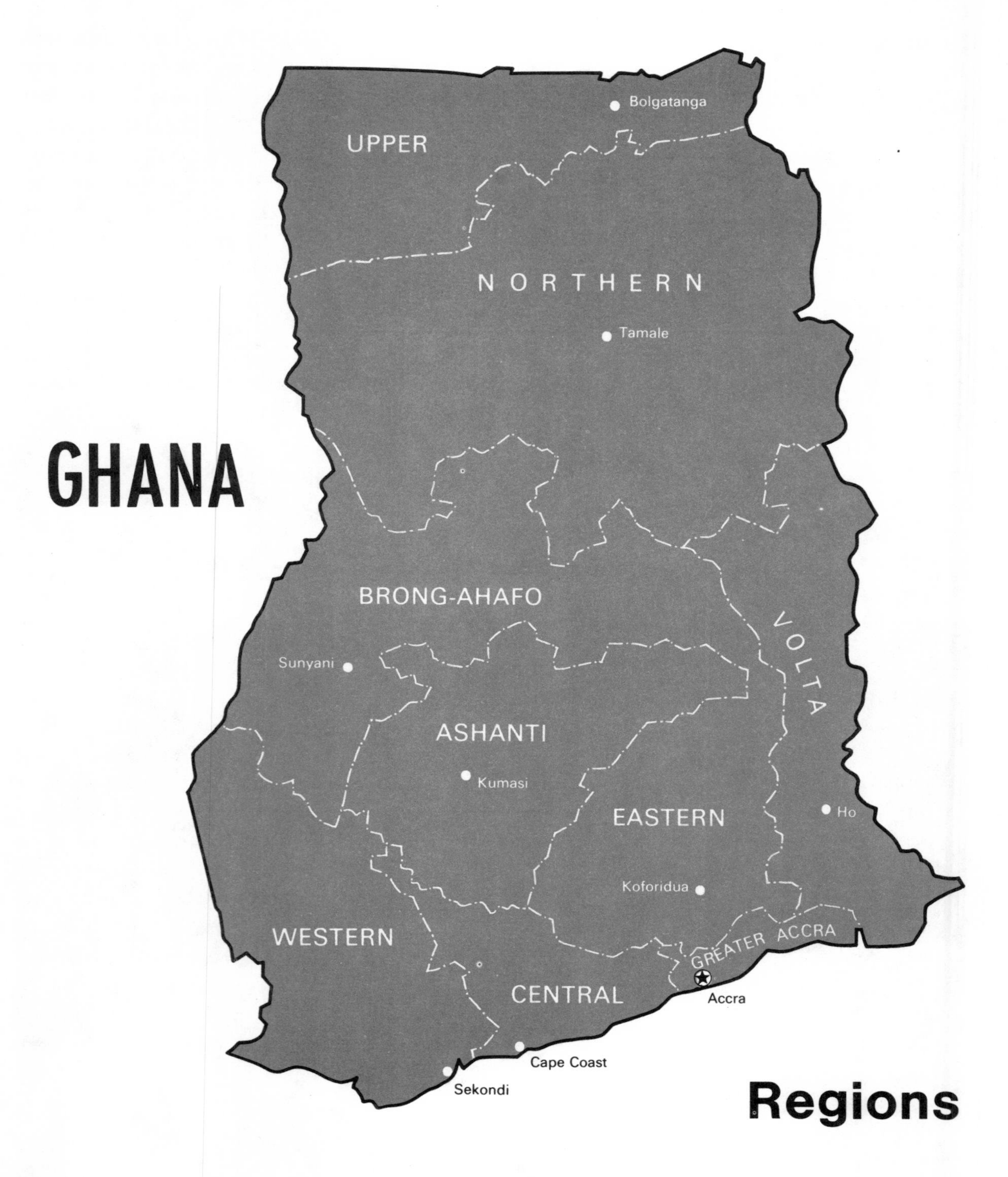
GHANA
Regions
Bolgatanga
UPPER
NORTHERN
Tamale
BRONG-AHAFO
VOLTA
Sunyani
ASHANTI
Kumasi
EASTERN
Ho
Koforidua
WESTERN
GREATER ACCRA
CENTRAL
Accra
Cape Coast
Sekondi

felt strongly that the country needed an alternative to the CPP. He became the leader of the United Party when it was formed in 1957. Disqualified from parliament during an overseas lecture tour, he traveled to a number of foreign universities in the next eight years as a visiting professor.

Dr. Busia returned to Ghana when the military coup took place in 1966 and formed the Progress Party. In the 1969 elections, Busia's Progress Party won 105 of the 140 National Assembly seats, making Busia prime minister.

After his election, Dr. Busia made plans to decentralize the government, hoping to meet the needs of the people in health, education, agriculture, and transportation. Buying and selling of goods was to be free of government restriction, except when necessary. Ghana was trying to develop both agriculture and industry, emphasizing agriculture. The country was on a very tight budget that prohibited or limited certain luxury items. By 1970, Ghana had achieved the highest per capita income (total national income divided by total population) in Africa—$294. With its many natural resources, its new Volta Dam power station, and its new government, it was hoped that political and economic stability could now be achieved.

1972—ARMY SEIZES POWER

Despite attempts by the Busia government to bring about economic stability to the country, great unrest was felt by many citizens in Ghana. While Dr. Busia was away in London for treatment of an eye ailment, junior Army officers led by 40-year-old Lt. Col. I. K. Acheampong nonviolently overturned the civilian government. The constitution was suspended, the parliament dissolved, and all political parties were banned. Once again, Dr. Busia was in exile.

Col. Acheampong quickly announced that the military government would be a temporary measure. The men established a twelve-man National Redemption Council (NRC) to tackle the important problems of the Ghanaian economy and national rule. This temporary governing body promised to turn over their power to a democratically elected government as soon as circumstances would permit them to do so.

DR. NKRUMAH COMES HOME

Not long after the 1972 military takeover in Ghana, Dr. Nkrumah, the exiled first leader of independent Ghana, died of cancer in a Rumanian hospital at the age of 62. Since 1966, he had been living in exile in Guinea. Now, the leaders in Ghana announced that they would bring Dr. Nkrumah's body home for burial. In describing Nkrumah, Dr. Azikiwe, the first president of Nigeria, said,

> "Much as we all may not have agreed with his ideas, he did his best to raise the stature of black men all over the world."

INTERNATIONAL RELATIONS

In the early days of independence, Dr. Nkrumah was very interested in bringing the people of Africa together in some united fashion. During a meeting with other leaders of African nations in 1963, Dr. Nkrumah advocated the formation of a United States of Africa. Although this did not actually occur, the Organization of African Unity was created in 1963, with Haile Selassie, then emperor of Ethiopia, as its first leader. Since 1963, Ghana has been an avid supporter of the OAU, as well as a member of the Commonwealth of Nations and the United Nations. In general, however, the government of Ghana has attempted to hold to a policy of non-alignment between East and West, and has asked other international leaders to respect this neutral position in world affairs.

EDUCATION

In the centuries before Europeans came to Ghana, children received all their education from their parents, grandparents, and other elders of their village. They learned the history of their people and how to get along as members of their group. When the first European-type school was introduced to the Gold Coast, few Africans were interested.

The United Nations flag is raised over the State House in 1958 to commemorate Ghana's first anniversary as a UN member and the opening of the UN Information Centre at Accra.

UNITED NATIONS

GHANA INFORMATION SERVICES

Children in Ghana go to school outdoors when the weather is very hot.

In the 1700s, as European traders began coming to the Gold Coast in greater numbers, more Africans became involved in trade with them. Urban areas grew along the coast. Many groups of Africans became quite rich on European trade. These merchants were the first Africans to see the advantage of a Western-type education. Some even sent their children to school in Europe.

Many Christian missionaries came to the Gold Coast between 1830 and 1850; the curriculum of the mission schools was basically limited to reading and writing English and learning arithmetic. Because these schools were the only schools available, the people who finished the course at the mission schools were considered quite educated and able to get such highly prestigious jobs as clerks, assistants to traders, catechists, or teachers, and jobs in government service. But the development of education in Ghana was largely confined to the coast throughout the nineteenth and early twentieth centuries. By 1930 more schools began to be opened in the Ashanti region, and attendance increased. Some mission stations had been opened in Ashanti after 1896. There had also been earlier efforts made to open

GHANA INFORMATION SERVICES

Above: Ghana's largest university is at Legon, just outside Accra. Opposite: Students study biology at a secondary school in Kumasi.

schools in the mid-nineteenth century, but these experiments were short-lived.

Today schools are scattered throughout much of Ghana. Children start school at the age of six. After six years, they go to middle school for a maximum of four years. When a middle school student thinks he is ready, he can take the extremely competitive exam for secondary school.

Secondary school lasts four years, and because people take the exam for it at different times, entering students range in age from twelve to seventeen. The best secondary schools (and the ones most students choose) are in Cape Coast, Accra, and Kumasi. Middle school students can also choose to go to teacher-training colleges or to technical institutes, rather than secondary school.

There are presently seven thousand students studying in Ghana's three universities: the University of Ghana at Legon (outside of Accra), the University of Cape Coast, and the University of Science and Technology, Kumasi. The university at Legon also includes Ghana Medical School.

JOHN MOSS/BLACK STAR

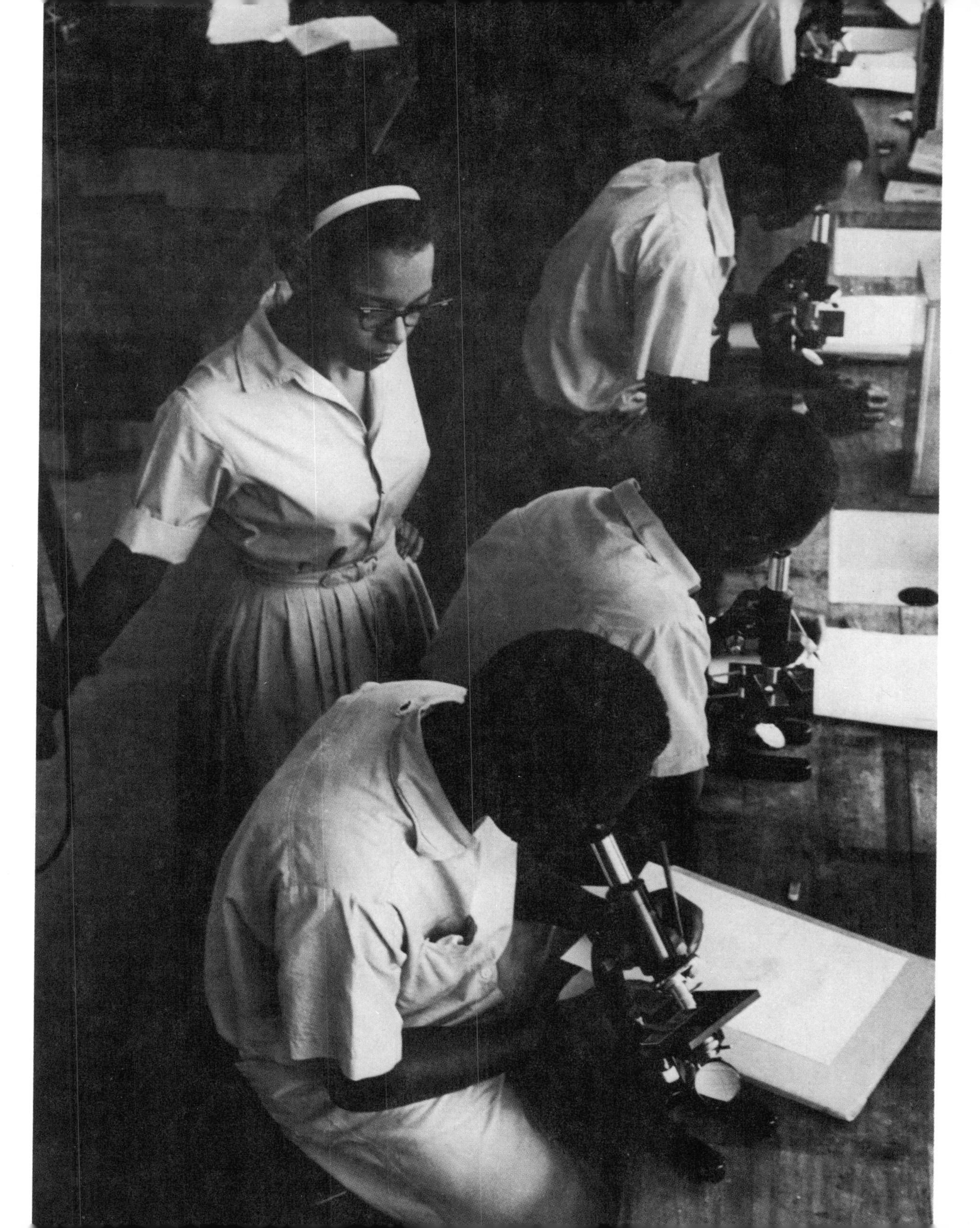

Natural Treasures

In earlier times the Gold Coast earned its reputation due to its vast deposits of gold hidden within the earth. Although not as important today for international trade, the gold of Ghana is still considered one of the nation's treasures. In addition, a number of other minerals, such as manganese, diamonds, and bauxite, are found in Ghana.

RIVERS AND OCEAN

Ghana's rivers and ocean teem with many natural treasures. Some of the finest fish of the entire African continent may be found in these waters. Men ply the rivers in their dugout canoes, veering around sleeping crocodiles, catching freshwater fish, and trapping crayfish. Along the coast, fishermen in dugout canoes throw out large nets called seines to catch afafa (horse mackerel). Alongside, porpoises, silver marlins, and large tuna swim in the clear blue water. The "two-pole" tuna is blue and silver and weighs as much as seventy pounds; men travel out in fishing boats to catch these protein-rich fish. In this part of the ocean also lives the manatee. Resembling the sea cow, this seal-like animal with a broad, rounded tail thrives on ocean plants.

Boti Falls is located at the village of Huhunya, near Koforidua, the capital of the Eastern Region.

GHANA INFORMATION SERVICES

FARM AND FOREST

The forest is rich in agricultural products, especially cocoa, palm oil, yams, plantain, beans, groundnuts (peanuts), wild rubber, mahogany, and kola nuts. Treetops two hundred feet high can be seen. The branches and leaves of the tall trees entwine to form a canopy, which shuts out the sunlight. Wawa or obeche, sapele, mahogany, and utile trees are found here; these trees are sought after for lumber.

Monkeys and chimpanzees swing from the vines. Hippopotamuses wallow in the muddy rivers, while crocodiles sleep along the riverbanks. Snails sluggishly crawl along the ground. Snakes weave in and out of the branches and between the giant ferns. Black ants move busily about, marching in columns. A pangolin digs for ants with its long, scaly nose, and guinea

Below: A girl plays with one of the crocodiles at the Sacred Crocodile Pond at Paga, Northern Region. The pond is a popular place for tourists to visit. Right: Two men examine a crop of cocoa pods.

GHANA INFORMATION SERVICES

GHANA INFORMATION SERVICES

Agriculture is very important in Ghana. Above: A woman harvests lush coffee plants. Left: This man is tapping a large rubber tree for its valuable sap. Below: A northern farm family with some of their cattle and hay.

UNITED NATIONS

GHANA INFORMATION SERVICES

hens scratch in the dirt for worms. Above, brightly colored parrots stand out from the green of the trees and turtledoves coo in the branches.

Ghana's savanna land and plains are also rich in different kinds of vegetation and wildlife. Millet, guinea corn, groundnuts, beans, rice, and yams grow plentifully here. The nut of the shea tree contains a pale colored, rich fat called shea butter, used for cooking and for making soap and candles. The savanna grasses are ideal cattle pasture, and many people in the north keep some cattle.

The Mole Game Reserve in northwestern Ghana protects some of the country's wildlife, such as antelope, gazelles, buffalo, elephants, servals, hunting dogs, and lions. Egrets, marabou, rhino birds, crested or crown cranes, whale-backed storks or shoebills, and the bald-headed ibis may also be seen here. Poisonous snakes and pythons are also known in the region.

Northern women collect shea nuts. They'll find many uses for the thick shea butter inside the nuts.

GHANA INFORMATION SERVICES

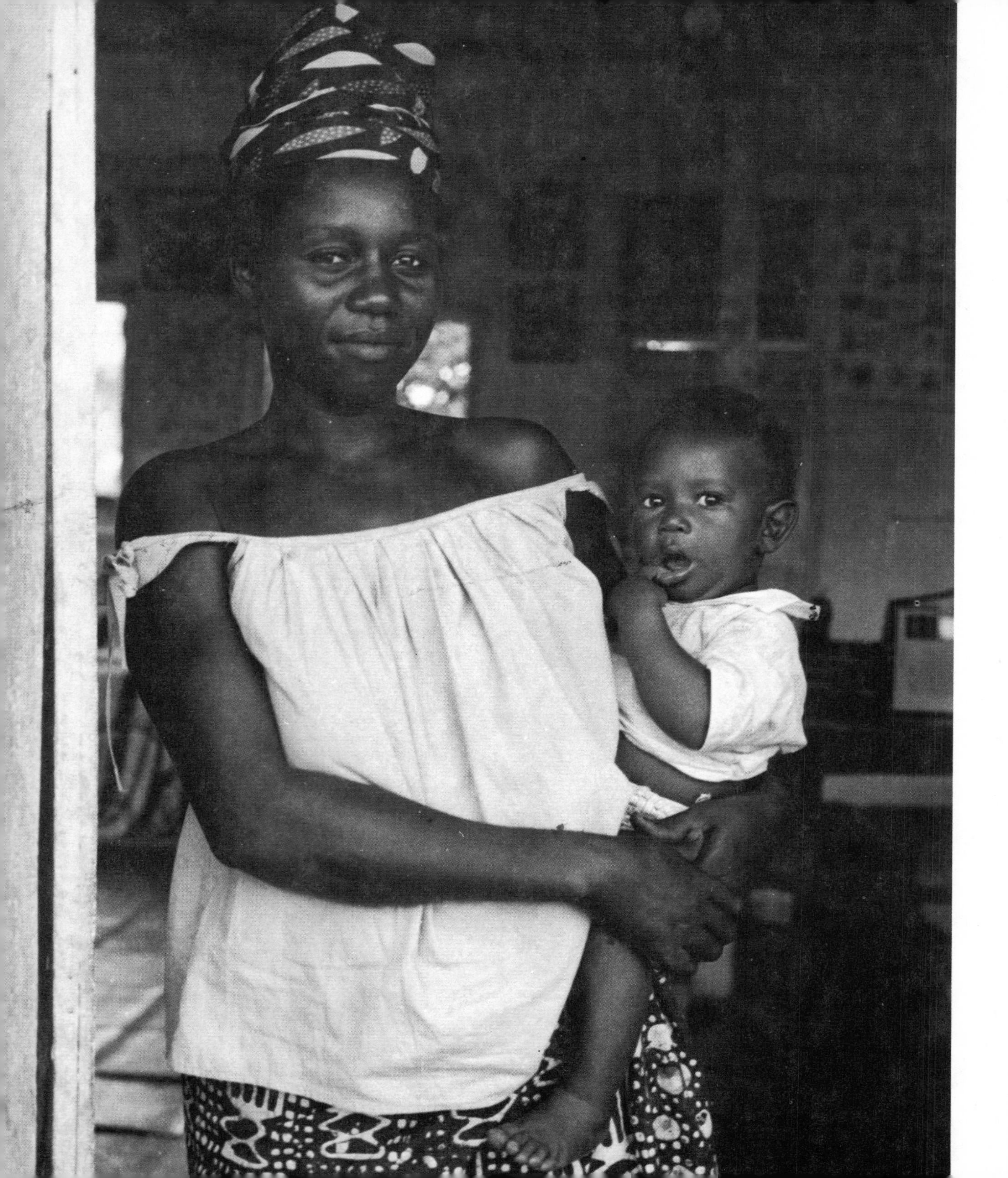

The People Live in Ghana

PEOPLE

Ghana's ten million people are divided into about fifty ethnic groups, each in a specific area of the country. The areas of densest population in Ghana are the coast and the Ashanti region, especially the cities of Accra and Kumasi. Yet 64 percent of the people live in rural settlements.

The Akan people make up 43 percent of the country's population. They live mostly in the forest country west of the Volta River. The Ashanti and the Fante are the two largest subgroups of the Akan.

After the Akan, the second most numerous people are the Ewe, who make up about 12.5 percent of the population. The grassy plain of Accra, between the Akan and the Ewe, is the home of the Ga and Adangbe peoples. Together, these two groups make up about 7 percent of the population.

The northern territories are occupied by a number of smaller ethnic groups known as the Northern Group. Altogether they make up about 28.8 percent of the population. Among the best known peoples in the Northern Group are the Dagomba, Gonja, and Mamprusi.

All of these ethnic groups are similar in their ways of life except for one thing —language. Among the major African languages in Ghana are Twi (Akan), Dagbani, Ewe, Ga-Adangbe, and Nzima.

This little boy and his mother live in Ghana's beautiful capital city, Accra.

UNITED NATIONS

English is the official and commercial language; it is taught in all schools. Now Akan, or Twi, as it is sometimes called, is also recognized as an official language. Thus, schoolchildren usually speak their "first" language, such as Twi, at home, but generally use English in their classroom.

RELIGION

About 60 percent of the people in Ghana still follow the religious beliefs of their ancestors, who saw the universe as occupied by personal spirits of all kinds. This kind of belief is called *animism.* As in Western religions, there is a Supreme Being (called "Nyame" by the Akan). But there are also a number of lesser deities, who are either connected with natural phenomena such as rain or trees, or with the cult of the ancestral spirits. Each ethnic group has its own set of deities. Religious beliefs are a constant part of everyday life, and are discussed and passed along in proverbs, common sayings, myths, poetry, and folklore.

Two of the world's major religions, Islam and Christianity, have also found many believers in Ghana. The Islamic religion began to spread slowly south from the Mali empire around 1400, and it

Traditional costumes for religious festivals are often very elaborate, like the one this boy is wearing.

GHANA INFORMATION SERVICES

Choir members sing during services at the Roman Catholic Church in Accra. GHANA INFORMATION SERVICES

reached the Gonja area around the sixteenth or seventeenth century. Soon it spread through northern Ghana and was accepted by many of the Dagomba and Mamprusi peoples, then moved farther south to the Ashanti. Today about 10 percent of the people in Ghana are Muslims. Most of them live in the north, but many live in Accra, Kumasi, and other large towns.

When European traders began arriving in Ghana, Christian missionaries were not far behind. Their work was never very successful until European-style schools were started. These were taught by missionaries who passed along religious ideas that were eagerly adopted. Today Christians make up 30 percent of Ghana's population.

It is important to understand that the Islamic and Christian religions as practiced in Ghana, and in much of Africa, are not exactly the same as elsewhere in the world. Traditional beliefs were too deeply entrenched in Ghana to eliminate or replace them. So the people to some extent integrated the beliefs and rituals of the new religion with their traditional beliefs.

Right: This northern woman is cutting up fruit from the dawadawa tree. Below: Bowls of shea butter are ready to be sold at the marketplace in Tamale.

GHANA INFORMATION SERVICES

FOODS

Due to the natural resources of the land, and partially due to the creative use made of the land, a wide variety of agricultural products are available to the people of Ghana. It is not surprising then to find people making interesting use of these products in their daily menus.

Fufu is one of the staple foods used by many people in Ghana. It can be made from yam, or cassava, cocoyam, or plantain. It is usually served as a standard accompaniment to stews or spicy soups and sauces.

In making fufu, the yam or plantain must first be peeled and cut into smaller slices. Once a sufficient quantity has been prepared, it is usually cooked in a pot of salted water. After reaching a boiling point, the contents are allowed to simmer for about forty-five minutes. The tender yams are then pounded into a soft paste, and reshaped into small balls. This makes them easy to handle for eating and dipping into sauces or stews.

Ghanaians often use red and green peppers to flavor their sauces and stews. Chicken, fish, and meats are used in combination with other vegetables to add to the variety of foodstuffs that one might encounter if visiting Ghana. Traditionally, most Ghanaians rely heavily upon the staples of plantain, yam, cassava, okra, or maize for most of their daily meals.

The numerous wild fruits and their leaves are used in many ways. The nut of the shea tree contains a fat called shea butter, which is used for cooking and soapmaking; oil is pressed out of palm nuts for use in cooking. Groundnuts are usually pounded to make a butter, eaten alone, or used in sauces.

The white yam that grows in Ghana is the "potato of Africa." White yams are so big that one of them can feed a whole family. To show the people's gratitude for this wonderful vegetable, yam feast days are celebrated. Among the Ashanti, yam dishes are served at ceremonies for birth, death, marriage, and recovery from an accident or disease.

Corn is a symbol of successful harvest to the Ga people. The great Ga feast called "Hooting at Hunger" honors the success of the year's harvest. This festival has colorful costumes and pageantry. *Kpekple* (a farina prepared from cornmeal and eaten with fish and palm-nut stew) is often served.

Eggs are symbols of fertility and triumph to the Ashanti. An old saying is: "The sun is but an egg that hatches great things."

TEXTILES

The art of weaving has been practiced in Ghana for many centuries. The same type of loom used centuries ago is still used today. In olden times, most of the weaving was done by men. Boys learned the technique of weaving at a young age and had to serve two- or three-year apprenticeships.

This boy is learning to weave at the Achimota school.

GHANA INFORMATION SERVICES

One of the most famous fabrics in Ghana is the kente cloth. "Kente" means "that which will not tear under any conditions." In kente weaving, narrow bands three to four inches wide, each with a different design, are woven of silk, then cut into small sections. The stripes, often with different designs, are sewn together on a cotton cloth base.

Originally, kente cloth was restricted to kings. Later, kings determined who could wear kente cloth. Traditionally, the design of the finished kente cloth told something of the wearer, such as clan, social status, or sex. For example, the *Agyengyenesu* ("setting down the disturbed sediments of muddy water") design symbolized a peacemaker; the *Embadda* design ("that which has never happened before") symbolized uniqueness. *Toku-Akyeratema* ("the royal soul's cloth") represented sanctity and purity. *Sika-futuru* ("gold dust") represented wealth and glory; and *Aberewa-Bene* ("a wise old woman") represented old age and wisdom.

Colors, too, were used symbolically, and only certain colors were worn on certain occasions. For example, white represented purity, joy, and victory; it was worn by young girls, brides, and those who had recovered from illness. Black or dark red represented the power of death and the

UNITED NATIONS

Ghana's kente *cloth has become world famous. Here professional weavers create this luxurious cloth with its beautiful and intricate designs.*

GHANA INFORMATION SERVICES

GHANA INFORMATION SERVICES

Above: Members of the Ghana Institute of Arts and Culture beat out ancient rhythms on their traditional drums. Right: The Golden Stool is the symbol of unity for the Ashanti people.

devil; it was worn during funeral ceremonies. Gold signified royalty and was worn by chiefs.

Today, anyone can wear any design, and kente cloth is the national costume of Ghana. But kente cloth is still quite valuable and expensive—each twelve-foot length of kente cloth costs $200 or more depending upon quality.

DRUMMING

Drumming in Ghana is not simply a matter of rhythms; rather, it is a language and an important form of communication. Drumming imitates the sounds of words. The spoken language is converted to musical phrases by a rhythm and a melody, through pitches, pauses, and speeds. The meaning regulates the rhythm.

A person who learns the drum language can play commands in short, loud drumbeats. One must learn simple sounds, how to call friends, how to play riddles, proverbs, and jokes, and how to speak like the animals in the forest.

Each drum has a specific name and use. The *etwie* (leopard) drum is carried over the shoulder. The drummer rubs the drumsticks back and forth across the surface of the drum skin, and the drum emits a sound like a snarling leopard. The etwie drum is beaten to show that the chief is brave and dangerous. It was used during wars to frighten away the enemy, who would think that a leopard was nearby.

Nkrawiri means "go say it and be killed." The Nkrawiri drum was beaten to summon people to court. In olden days, it was beaten for people who were sentenced to death.

Mpebi means "I don't like any." This drum was beaten for someone who broke a customary law.

Today, drums in Ghana are also used in drum orchestras. Each kind of orchestra is made of a different combination of drums, with distinctive rhythms, combined with horns and gongs.

THE ASANTEHENE

Nearly half of the Africans in Ghana are members of the Akan people. Included among the Akan are the very numerous Ashanti. Each group of Ashanti has its own chief, and the ceremonial ruler of all the chiefs is the Asantehene, or king.

The office of Asantehene, and the power and dignity of that office, are known as the stool, much as the monarchy in England is known as the throne. Though no one, including the Asantehene, ever actually sits on the Golden Stool, the "throne" of the Asantehene is a stool made of wood, with gold ornamentation.

When the stool becomes vacant, a new Asantehene must be chosen. The *krontihene* (in the old days, head of the Kumasi army and next in rank to the Asantehene) calls a meeting of the *oman*, or the people of the area ruled by the chief. During the meeting, the krontihene sends the linguist to the queen mother with this message: "The oman are assembled and you are

Nana Opuku Ware II was installed as Asantehene, leader of the Ashanti, in 1970.

GHANA INFORMATION SERVICES

asked to nominate a candidate to occupy the stool." The queen mother is given three chances to nominate a candidate. If all three fail to qualify, the oman can nominate a candidate for the queen mother's approval.

In ceremonial matters, the Asantehene does not rule alone, though he does have final say. He takes much advice from the Asantehemaa or queen mother (usually his own mother or sister, the highest ranking woman in the royal family), from senior chiefs, or from the "linguists," or spokesmen.

During the summer of 1970, a new Asantehene was enstooled. Crowds of almost 100,000 people watched as Mr. Jacob Matthew Poku became the leader of the Ashanti. His official Asantehene name is Nana Opoku Ware II. His queen mother is Amma Sewaa Nyaako.

Before his enstoolment, Mr. Poku was the ambassador-designate to Italy. In the past he also held the post of commissioner of transport and communications during the time of the National Liberation Council. Mr. Poku was educated in Ghana, and studied at the Middle Temple, London, to become a lawyer.

Asantehenes do not communicate directly with their people, but instead speak to a man called a linguist, who passes the Asantehene's word to the people and in turn passes the people's response and feelings to the Asantehene. In the old days the linguist also had important administrative functions in the executive branch of government.

THE ENSTOOLMENT CEREMONY

On the day of the enstoolment, a solemn and pompous ceremony takes place in the midst of drumming and dancing. A procession follows each chief. The man behind each chief carries over his head a carved wooden stool—the symbol of that chief's authority and power.

Everywhere in the square is the gleam of gold, for gold treasures are brought out on such occasions. Rifles, knives, and pouches of the Asantehene's bodyguard are covered with gold. The chiefs hold their swords of state at waist level; on the carved hilts of the swords are gold animals. Gold jewelry shines from the folds of the chiefs' robes, which are made of brightly colored kente cloth. The chiefs are shielded from the hot sun by large, colorful umbrellas. In the background, hundreds of drums sound in rhythm.

The climax of the ceremony comes when the new Asantehene swears the oath of allegiance. He then sits on a wooden stool, and the people parade to the seat of the Asantehene and prostrate themselves by kneeling on the ground.

The Asantehene has many, many people in his court.

GHANA INFORMATION SERVICES

THE QUEEN MOTHER

The queen mother is considered "the daughter of the moon"; her son is considered "the son of the sun." Legend says that long ago an Asantehene and his sister tried to equal in splendor the heavenly bodies—the sun and the moon. On evenings of the new moon, the queen, dressed in white robes and silver jewelry, danced in the moonlight. Upon her death, her body was covered with silver. Thus began the institution of the queen mother. When gold was later discovered in great quantities, gold replaced silver in ceremonial uses.

According to tradition, the queen mother is expected to be as calm and peaceful as the moon. She must carry all the qualities desired in the womanhood of her people. The queen mother's main duty is to act as the Asantehene's adviser in matters concerning the welfare of women. Chiefs and counselors also turn to her for advice. The queen mother knows who are the members of the ruling clan and the proper order of succession. The queen mother is consulted when the history of the people must be traced.

Thus, the queen mother holds a position equal to, but different from that of the Asantehene. Throughout history, queen mothers have set noble examples. In 1900, when the Asantehene was deported, the queen mother of Ejisu, Yaa Asantewa, led the Ashanti armies against the British. She is still remembered as one of Ghana's greatest heroines.

THE ROLE OF WOMEN

The role of women in Ghana has become increasingly important. Not only have the Akan people traditionally held their queen mother in high regard, but since the days of Dr. Nkrumah, women have begun to assume more important roles in the modern development of the nation.

Women are to be found in many professions, such as medicine, law, and politics. The government protects the equality of the sexes, and guarantees equal pay for equal services. However, the government in Ghana has advanced its concern for family women by providing maternity welfare, prohibiting night work, and encouraging the development of well-equipped day nurseries that cater to children of working women.

FOLKLORE

Ghana is rich in folklore and in legend. Each ethnic group has its own legends that are part of that group's history. Sometimes

Local Ashanti chiefs are directly responsible to the Asantehene. The umbrella is a symbol of the chief's authority. Like the Asantehene, chiefs have spokesmen, or linguists, *to bring their wishes and commands to the people.*

these legends say that supernatural or spiritual events took place that changed the course of history. But always these events can be explained by the group religion. For example, Ashanti legend tells of the priest, Okomfo Anokye, who was said to have brought down the Golden Stool from the sky.

Folktales are an important part of Ghana's culture. Many of the country's folktales are about Anansi, the spider. He is the hero of many of the folk stories. In olden days, every evening was spent storytelling. Children would sit spellbound in the evening light, fascinated by the tales. This tradition is still carried on, especially in the rural north. Before formal education came to Ghana, storytelling was the way children received an education. Many of the stories told of the group's history, and folktales taught religious beliefs and morals.

Proverbs and slogans are also important in Ghanaian society. Proverbs are used in everyday speech. The meanings of proverbs are generally understood by all the people. In the olden days, a man who could speak well was one who used many proverbs in his conversation. The proverbs came from the stories, legends, and folktales handed down through the ages.

Today, written slogans are common sights in Ghana. It is not known when the practice of displaying slogans on vehicles, walls, and other places began. The writer of the slogan is simply expressing an experience or a philosophy of life. Such slogans as "All days are not equal," "Good mother," "Love your enemies," "Simplicity," and "God is wonderful" appear throughout the country.

Ghanaians are proud of their heritage, and that pride is reflected in the nation. Traditional ceremonies are still held; and chiefs and queen mothers are respected. Even though the nation is quickly becoming industrialized, Ghana has not forgotten its heritage and traditions.

The People Work in Ghana

Ever since 1968, Ghana's balance of trade has been positive: the country exports more than it imports. Ghana trades mostly with the United Kingdom, the European Economic Community (EEC), the United States, and Eastern Bloc nations. Its main imports are food, mineral feeds, chemicals, manufactured goods, machinery, and transport equipment. Its main exports are cocoa, logs and timber, and gold and other minerals.

AGRICULTURE

Ghana's economy is mainly agricultural; in fact, 65 percent of the nation's exports are provided by one agricultural product alone—cocoa. Ghana produces more cocoa than any other nation in the world. Cacao trees are grown, their pods fermented, and the seeds (cocoa beans) are dried and roasted in the sun. The seeds are then manufactured into cocoa. One third of Ghana's population earn their living from this product.

Although it is good to have such a profitable export product, the government realizes the danger of reliance on one product. The money Ghana earns on exports can fluctuate greatly depending on the world market price of cocoa. And a tree disease could wipe out the crop. In the 1940s, for example, a virus called swollen shoot, carried by the mealybug, spread quickly throughout the land, killing cacao trees as it went. In order to stop this virus, the government had to burn and cut down many trees.

At present, Ghana's main food crops are maize, rice, sorghum, millet, yams, cassava, and plantain. All of these foods are very important in the Ghanaian diet, but

GHANA INFORMATION SERVICES

Ghanaians do not grow enough of these products to feed the entire country. Thus, food products must also be imported. The government plans to expand production of these products in order to make the country agriculturally self-sufficient.

Ghana has a small canning industry but needs to grow its own vegetables and fruits, such as tomatoes, lemons, oranges, and pineapples. Other crops the government hopes to expand include kinaf (for the fiber industry), tobacco, rubber, and cotton.

Cattle and other livestock are raised by many farmers, and in some areas the livestock are considered status symbols—as in much of Africa. Though Ghanaians sometimes use a few of their animals for food, they do not like to sell any of the family herd. However, the government is trying to encourage the raising of livestock for sale so that the standard of living can be improved. Livestock ranches are being developed for this purpose.

INDUSTRIES

Presently in operation in Ghana are textile factories, breweries, flour mills, sugar factories, a cement factory, canneries, and other similar industries. Most

UNITED NATIONS

Opposite: Tomato farming is a growing industry in the north. Above: Some of the timber from the forests that cover almost half the country is brought to the rail yards at Kumasi for shipment elsewhere.

of these industries depend on the importation of raw materials.

Forest products account for 8.5 percent of Ghana's exports. The forests, which cover almost half the country's land surface, contain over 150 species of timber. Wawa or opeche, sapele, mahogany, and utile trees are highly valued for their wood. Most of this wood is exported in the form of logs or sawn timber, but there are a few plants that produce plywood and veneers (in which a layer of superior wood is glued to inferior wood).

Some of the finest fish in Africa are found in Ghana's rivers and in the Gulf of Guinea. Along the coast, fishermen catch tuna, afafa, talapia, and carp in small fishing boats and dugout canoes. Fish is a popular food in Ghana, especially in the coastal regions.

GOLDSMITHS

Ghana's mineral exports are primarily in gold; Ghana is the world's fifth-largest producer of gold.

In early Ghana, goldsmiths were held in high esteem for their creative ability to transform this natural mineral into works of art. They were commissioned for special jobs by chiefs, traders, and other rich citizens who wanted to own as much gold as possible, for gold objects enhanced the dignity and increased the status of anyone wealthy enough to own them.

Goldsmiths are still important and highly respected in Ghana. In almost every town there is a goldsmith engaged in this centuries-old craft. Often a father teaches the craft to his son, who later inherits the tools and gold weights. Today, goldsmiths make men's jewelry such as rings, armlets, studs, earrings, charms, cufflinks, and pins, and women's jewelry such as bracelets, finger rings, necklaces, hairpins, waist bangles, and hair and ankle chains. Goldsmiths also make ornamental emblems and gold-plated figures molded in traditional designs.

Ghana's two other important export minerals are manganese and diamonds. Ghana is the world's third-largest producer of manganese and the world's third-largest producer, by weight, of diamonds. Most of Ghana's diamonds are used for industry rather than jewelry.

POWER

In 1961 the Volta River Authority (VRA) was established to build a power station on the Volta River, to control the resulting lake and the development of fishing and transport, and to promote the health and welfare of the people in the area.

A dam was built across the Volta River at Akosombo to create a vast body of water that would be used to generate hydroelectricity. The first of its kind in Africa, this project was completed in 1965. Its power output of 768,000 kilowats could provide abundant power for industrial growth in Ghana.

TRANSPORTATION

Roads are the most widely used form of transportation in Ghana. Now there are about seven thousand miles of principal roads in Ghana; about thirty-five hundred miles of hard-surfaced roads can be used throughout the year. Ghana's road system forms a network that centers on Kumasi, and is most complete in the south, where most of the people live.

Railroads are still confined to the southern half of the country and used primarily for transporting minerals and agricultural products to ships and in the harbors. The railway circles through the country from Kumasi to Takoradi, Kumasi to Accra, and through Achiasi in the coastal hinterland.

Canoes are the main form of transport on the rivers, and not much has been done to change this situation since the development of roads and the railway. It is impossible to navigate larger vessels up the whole length of any river, due to the rivers' shallow depth. Larger ferries and ferry boats are now used on Lake Volta.

The Ghana Airway Corporation handles flights within the country, as well as daily services along the west coast of

GHANA INFORMATION SERVICES

Ghana's government operates a large bus system. Buses are the principal means of travel throughout the country.

Africa. Airports are located in Tamale, Kumasi, Takoradi, and Accra. Accra has an international airport, where foreign airlines as well as Ghana Airways connect Ghana with other parts of the world.

Ghana's seaports are used mainly for large shipping lines. There is a minimum of passenger traffic. Ghana's government-owned line is called the Black Star Line. Each year, more than a thousand ships visit the ports of Tema, built in 1962, and Takoradi, built in 1928. These two ports handle the country's overseas trade. Takoradi exports mainly timber and minerals; the bulk of the cocoa is exported from Tema.

COMMUNICATIONS

Postal, telegraph, and telephone facilities are restricted to relatively few towns and do not extend to many rural areas.

Throughout the country, people own shortwave radios. Radios are an important means of bringing news quickly to rural areas.

Television is becoming increasingly popular, although reception is limited to the urban areas.

Ghana's main newspapers are the *Ashanti Pioneer*, the *Daily Graphic*, and the government-controlled *Ghanaian Times*.

The Enchantment of Ghana

THE NORTH

The northern part of Ghana remains rather isolated. This is a part of Africa that has had only about fifty years' contact with Western civilization. There are few modern buildings, no industry, and no railroad. The largest town in the north is Tamale, with a population of about 100,000.

The plains of the north are nearly flat; occasional trees and clumps of bushes are scattered in the savanna. Animals still run wild here; antelope roam freely and snakes slide through the tall grass.

Rural settlements are scattered throughout the plains, but the population is densest near the waterways. Near the settlements are fields planted with grains such as maize and millet, and vegetables such as yams, cassava, tomatoes, and groundnuts. Cattle wander about the grasses, sometimes accompanied by a boy. In the compounds, women pound yams with mortars and pestles and cook sauces in cast-iron pots over open fires.

Market day is one of the few times people in the north get together. Farmers come into town with wagons or bicycles overflowing with produce. Women walk the many miles to market, heavily laden with fresh vegetables and grains in woven baskets on top of their heads. They balance the baskets with one hand as they follow overgrown trails.

In the marketplace, merchants lay out their produce in neat piles on burlap bags or on blankets. Some merchants sit on the

Yendi women return home with pots of water from the community well.

GHANA INFORMATION SERVICES

ground, some squat, and others sit on small, wooden stools as they wait for customers. The colors of the market are bright and varied: women wear blouses and skirts of colorfully designed fabric and wear scarves wrapped around their heads. Their jewelry of gold and other metals glitters in the sunlight.

The sounds and smells of the market are as varied as the colors. Women haggle over prices and laugh, children shout, babies cry, chickens squawk, and cattle moo—all at the same time. In the background is the powerful rhythm of drums played by musicians praising the people using the market. The aroma is a combination of fresh produce, fish, and spices.

WHERE THE ASHANTI LIVE

Central Ghana is an area of thickly forested, hilly country. This is cocoa and timber land. Cacao trees share the forest with sapele trees and giant mahogany. Colorful birds flit through the trees as occasional huge pythons wrap their bodies around the branches. Below, small animals and insects hide in the thickly tangled growth.

This busy market is at the town of Yendi, located near Tamale, which is the largest town in the north.
GHANA INFORMATION SERVICES

GHANA INFORMATION SERVICES

Kumasi, the capital city of Ashanti Region, is a bustling and prosperous place.

This is Ashanti country—a land of peoples united by the Golden Stool.

The capital of Ashanti land is Kumasi—a city of about 340,000 people. Often called the "garden city," Kumasi has many parks and graceful streets. The city's magnet is Manhyia Palace, the residence of the Asantehene. Twenty-one miles southeast of Kumasi is Ghana's only natural lake, Lake Bosumtwi—a sacred lake surrounded by thick, forested highlands.

Nearby is Asantemanso—once a city, now a hamlet of only four houses. Asantemanso lies in a patch of thick, untouched forest, where no unauthorized person can enter without permission. It is patrolled constantly lest this taboo be broken. As the traditional Ashanti place of origin, Asantemanso is one of the most sacred places in the country.

ALONG THE COAST

The heavy surf pounds against the shore, bringing countless small bait fish to the surface. Men throw lines of bait fish behind their fishing boats to tempt the tuna following in the boat's wake.

UNITED NATIONS

Many coastal villages look like this one (above). In the foreground are oval ovens used to dry fish. Overlooking the village is an ancient Portuguese fort. Opposite top: One of Ghana's many popular beaches. Opposite bottom: Elmina Castle, built by the Portuguese in 1492, overlooks Elmina Beach.

On the shore, a fleet of dugout canoes are lined up, each marked with its purchase price. The canoes are colorfully decorated in black, red, white, and blue. A merchant jumps over the canoes, stepping on their woven seats, as he shows the boats to a customer. Only a few feet away, children play in the sand. Behind the sandy shoreline are faded wooden houses. In the village market, clams and other shellfish dry in the sun. Such fishing villages are scattered along Ghana's coastline, interrupted occasionally by large towns that often surround ancient castles.

African slaves were once an important export of the Gold Coast. Prisoners by the hundreds were herded toward the slave pens of the large coastal forts, where they waited in crowded dungeons to be sold as slaves to wealthy Europeans or Americans.

Huge Elmina Castle dominates the coastline for miles. Built by the Portuguese in 1482, it was lost to the Dutch in 1637 and bought by Great Britain in 1872. There is a drawbridge over a dry moat and a twenty-foot tunnel through solid walls. Arched doorways lead to the dungeon and the barracks. Though Elmina is only one of many forts that dot the country's beautiful coastline, it is Ghana's oldest and largest.

GHANA INFORMATION SERVICES

MICHAEL ROBERTS

Accra's magnificent Arch of Independence is one of the capital's newest and most famous landmarks.

THE CAPITAL

Accra has grown from a sleepy colonial capital to a modern, well-planned city of over 660,000 people. Trees, shrubs, and flowers line the wide streets. Shopping centers have large department stores and fashionable boutiques. Ghana Museum is a modern circular building. In the new part of Accra is the Arch of Independence. Outside the city is the University of Ghana, attended by thousands of students.

Accra's nightlife is lively, with many open-air movies, restaurants, nightclubs, and dance halls. The sounds of the city are unique: a blend of African music and the rhythms of calypso, samba, and blues.

Mixed in with this modern city are remnants of the earliest days of European settlement. Old castles and forts still stand. The seventeenth-century English and Dutch forts are now used as prisons, and the Danish fort Christianborg now houses the office of the head of state.

In the harbors of old Accra the scene has also changed from its old ways. Accra's port is closed. All ships now dock at Tema to the east. But local fishermen in dugout canoes and with large nets still use this surf port.

There are indeed many changes throughout this nation. The people hope these changes will continue to bring a better way of life for all of Ghana.

Handy Reference Section

INSTANT FACTS

Political:

Official Name—Republic of Ghana
Capital—Accra (ah-KRAH)
Official Languages—English and Akan
Literacy Rate—25 percent literate in English
Religions—60 percent animist; 30 percent Christian; 10 percent Muslim
Flag—Three horizontal stripes (top to bottom): red, gold, and green. In the center of the gold stripe is a black star. Red represents independence, gold stands for wealth, green represents forest and farms, and the star symbolizes African freedom.

Geographical:

Area—92,100 square miles
Greatest Length—445 miles
Greatest Width—310 miles
Highest Point—Mount Afadjoto (2,905 feet)
Lowest Point—Sea level

POPULATION

Total Population (1976 estimate)—10,188,000
Population Growth Rate—2.8 percent
Population Density—111 persons per square mile

Population Distribution (ethnic):

Group	*Percent*
Akan	43.0
Northern Group	28.8
Ewe	12.5
Ga	3.6
Adangbe	3.0
Other	9.1

Major Cities:

Accra	663,880
Kumasi	342,986
Sekondi-Takoradi	161,071

REGIONS

Region	*Capital*
Ashanti	Kumasi
Brong-Ahafo	Sunyani
Central	Cape Coast
Eastern	Koforidua
Greater Accra	Accra
Northern	Tamale
Upper	Bolgatanga
Volta	Ho
Western	Sekondi

YOU HAVE A DATE WITH HISTORY

600 B.C.—Iron working becomes known in West Africa
1000-1200 A.D.—Ghana empire
1470—Portuguese visit Da Mina (Elmina) on Gold Coast
1481—Portuguese build fort at Elmina
1642—Dutch take control of Portuguese trade areas
1690s—Golden Stool comes to Ashanti nation
1807—England forbids slavery
1817—Ashanti negotiate first treaty with Africa Company
1821—Africa Company abolished by British government
1874—British-Ashanti conflict; Treaty of Fomena; Gold Coast colony created as a result of treaty
1896—British military occupation of Ashanti

1900—Yaa Asantewa War

1902—Ashanti nation annexed to crown colony

1914—Gold Coast becomes richest colonial possession of England

1918—National Congress of British West Africa founded

1935—Popular press movement established for Africans in Gold Coast

1947—Kwame Nkrumah returns to Gold Coast

1950—Peaceful strike and boycott by Africans against colonial government

1954—Nkrumah and party gain political leadership in transition government

1956—"Hour of Triumph" (September 17)

1957—Independence Day (March 6)

1960—Ghana becomes a republic

1966—Coup d'état overthrows Nkrumah (February 24)

1969—Dr. Kofi Abrefa Busia becomes prime minister

1970—Nana Opoku Ware II becomes Asantehene

1972—Col. Acheampong and military assume military control of government (January 13)

1974—"Keep Right" day (August 4)

Index

Page numbers with asterisks following indicate illustrations.

About the Authors

With the publication of his first book for school use when he was twenty, **Allan Carpenter** began a career as an author that has spanned more than 135 books—with more still to be published in the Enchantment of Africa series for Childrens Press. After teaching in the public schools of Des Moines, Mr. Carpenter began his career as an educational publisher at the age of twenty-one when he founded the magazine *Teachers Digest*. In the field of educational periodicals, he was responsible for many innovations. During his many years in publishing, he has perfected a highly organized approach to handling large volumes of factual material: after extensive traveling and having collected all possible materials, he systematically reviews and organizes everything. From his apartment high in Chicago's John Hancock Building, Allan recalls: "My collection and assimilation of materials on the states and countries began before the publication of my first book." Allan is the founder of Carpenter Publishing House and of Infordata International, Inc., publishers of *Issues in Education* and *Index to U.S. Government Periodicals*. When he is not writing or traveling, his principal avocation is music. He has been the principal bassist of many symphonies, and he managed the country's leading non-professional symphony for twenty-five years.

Co-author **James W. Hughes** has traveled extensively through over half of the nations of Africa and lived and worked in Kenya for several years. Dr. Hughes has contributed to journals and books in both Africa and the United States. He has served as chairman of the International Activities Committee of the National Council for the Social Studies, and has served as an educational consultant for the International Relations Committee of the National Education Association in both Kenya and Nepal. Dr. Hughes is currently Director of Teacher Education at Oakland University.